A TIME TO PREPARE

A Practical Guide for Individuals and Families
in Determining A Jewish Approach to Making
Personal Arrangements, Establishing the
Limits of Medical Care and Embracing Rituals at the End of Life

Edited by Rabbi Richard F. Address

J E W I S H
F A M I L Y
CONCERNS

Creating Caring Congregations

UAHC Press
New York, New York

Acknowledgements

Grateful appreciation for helping with this revision to Rabbi Terry Bard, Dr. Harvey Gordon, Mr. Steven Burkett, Esq., Mr. Jerome Apfel, Esq., Rabbi "Jake" Jackofsky, Rabbi Dan Freelander, and from the UAHC Press: Ken Gesser, Liane Broido, Elyssa Mosbacher, and Debra Hirsch Corman. Thanks also to Dr. Linda Emanuel for her permission to use the updated Advance Directive, and a friend of this project, Esther Rhode (z'l).

We are grateful to the Central Conference of American Rabbis, the New Jersey Bio-ethics Commission and Susan Casid for continuing use of material in this revision. Likewise, to Al Vorspan, Arthur Grant and Rabbi Bernard Zlotowitz, our thanks for being so helpful with previous editions of *A Time To Prepare*.

Special thanks to Marcia Hochman and the Jewish Family Concerns chairs: Jean Abarbanel, Marshall Zolla and Mike Grunebaum.

Initial printing of this document was made possible
through the estate of Mr. Martin Address (z'l)
**

A Time to Prepare is a publication of The Union of American
Hebrew Congregations Department of Jewish Family Concerns

Jean Abarbanel, Chair
Marshall Zolla, Vice Chair
Mike Grunebaum, Vice Chair
Dr. Harvey Gordon, Chair, Bio-ethics Committee
Rabbi Richard F. Address, D.Min., Director
Marcia Hochman, MSW, LCSW, Assistant Director

Contents

Introduction

"Birth is a beginning and death a destination. . .and life is a journey."

The journey of life is one of wonder and joy, as well as frustration and grief. Helping people cope with the reality of life's end is one of Judaism's greatest gifts. Often the death of a loved one is overwhelming. The decisions that have to be made regarding the events that lead up to, surround, and follow a funeral can often be a source of great stress, and decisions created by medical technology often add to that stress. This manual was created to help individuals anticipate many of these decisions and to view the process through appropriate Jewish eyes.

The idea for this manual originated with Susan Casid of Temple Shalom in Dallas, Texas. The sudden death of her husband, Gerald, made her realize the importance of having a personal record of one's life and statement of wishes, to save those who remain the stress of trying to reconstruct a personal history of the deceased. Susan created a document for Temple Shalom, writing of the necessity of using such a workbook to spare survivors the "added weight of confusion on top of their grief." She noted in her introduction that, "You can give your loved ones this gift of freedom and time to work through the grieving process if you arrange your affairs by completing the enclosed workbook. Life insurance and a will are simply not enough. This completed workbook is truly one of the most important presents you will ever give your loved ones."

The UAHC received permission from Susan to expand her initial idea. We have added appropriate material from Jewish sources, hoping to answer anticipated questions about how contemporary Judaism can guide the making of sacred decisions at life's end in light of medical technology's advances. In recent years there has been increased attention given to dealing with issues such as Advance Directives for Medical Care (so-called "living wills"), Powers of Attorney for Health Care and organ donation. Longevity and technology have given rise to an increasing number of options for care and treatment. *A Time To Prepare* incorporates forms that allow you to use this document as a comprehensive family workbook. We have also found that many of our congregations, through their Caring

Community or Family Concerns committees, have used this workbook as a text around which to develop a multi-session education program on end-of-life decisions.

In any of these discussions, consultation with your rabbi is essential. Likewise, given the varieties of jurisdiction, it is also advisable to consult with legal counsel to be aware of any changes in state or provincial positions.

It is not unusual that as the flame of life flickers down, there exists a balancing of issues and interests. Profound spiritual moments are often presented. Opportunities for reflection, blessing and reconciliation often emerge. The discussions of how someone wishes to be treated at life's end provide the family with moments of sacred potential. Respect for and the dignity of the patient is of a high priority and is rooted in our tradition. The need for sincere and honest, Jewish, value-oriented discussions of the issues surrounding medical care can help eliminate what some see as conflicting interests. Marshall Zolla, Jewish Family Concerns vice-chair and practicing attorney, writes that in addition to the families' interests in proper care-giving, "The state has an interest in protecting its citizens from premature death. The medical profession has an interest in protecting its integrity and ensuring that scarce medical resources are put to the best uses. Finally, the judicial system, in the absence of direct legislative guidance, has an interest in ensuring that existing legal standards are not violated in the pursuit of conflicting interests."

(Marshall S. Zolla and Deborah Elizabeth Zolla, "Lasting Wishes," *Los Angeles Lawyer* 23, no. 9 (December 2000): 44.)

In addition to Life Data, Advance Directive and Resources, *A Time To Prepare* includes a section that encourages the creation of an ethical will. Within our tradition the concept of the "ethical will" is seen as equally important as the usual "material" will. This spiritual, moral, and ethical legacy is a sacred tradition, well worth the time and consideration.

Likewise, we have included some brief thoughts regarding Reform Judaism and its approach to decision making at the end of life. A resources section lists a wide variety of selections that will assist you, your family, and your congregation in further study.

It is our hope that you and the members of your family will make use of this document. Our tradition teaches that our most fundamental value is the dignity and sanctity of human life, a value that extends even unto death. We feel that proper use of this document can help you honor that fundamental value as you and your loved ones proceed on that journey from birth to death.

Please do not forget that once completed, copies of the forms expressing one's wishes should be placed in locations that can be accessed with some ease. Not only should copies be placed with your rabbi, lawyer, physician, and in your safe-deposit box, but also it is suggested that a copy be placed within a fire-proof box at home.

Finally, we have included a brief selection of traditional prayers and blessings that may help in rituals of saying good-bye. Religion teaches some of the greatest lessons about life through the rituals surrounding death. In his classic work, *Peace of Mind,* Joshua Loth Leibman recognizes this fact. He writes that on the one hand, religion gives comfort by fostering belief that the dead have passed from this life to a higher, transcendent level of existence. "On the other hand, it summons the survivors educated by tragedy, to accept anew the blessings and the burdens of earthly life. Thus Judaism and its rituals can allow us to confront the challenges of our journey. . .the tragic fragility of our brief day on earth and the reassertion of the value of that day in spite of its fragility."

The purpose of this manual is to help you confront the mystery of life's fragile journey. As we read on *Kol Nidrei* night in the *Gates of Repentance*:

> *Birth is a beginning*
> *And death is a destination*
> *And life is a journey, a sacred pilgrimage—*
> *To life everlasting.*
>
> ALBERT FINE

Rabbi Richard F. Address, D.Min.
UAHC Department of Jewish Family Concerns

2

Life Data

To the Person Filling Out the Workbook

1. Fill out this workbook in pencil so that it is kept current. Please remember to consult your attorney to keep abreast of changes in laws.

2. The information in this workbook should be reviewed regularly and appropriate corrections should be made.

3. Important papers should be kept in one place to facilitate the task facing your survivors.

4. Document carefully on the following pages the location of those papers. *Do not forget that notification of the location of keys and combinations is of equal importance.*

5. If a safe-deposit or at-home fire-proof lock box has been used to store any of the vital documents, be sure that you, as well as a designated cosigner, are authorized to have access to the box and that both people retain a key. Be sure that your bank or safe-deposit box company agrees that the box will be accessible to the surviving cosigner.

6. In addition to relatives and friends, many groups, agencies, firms, and administrations must be notified about death. Current telephone numbers of those who are to be notified immediately should be listed on pages 8–11, while the addresses and telephone numbers of organizations should be listed on pages 22–25.

7 When a new telephone book is delivered, check if the addresses and telephone numbers for Social Security, Veteran's Administration, Motor Vehicle Department, or any others have changed.

8. When your insurance policy renewals arrive, check that the policy numbers, addresses, and telephone numbers are still the same.

9. It will help your survivors if you write your obituary in advance or at least prepare a list of information. Space on page 14 has been provided for this purpose. You may want to look at the obituary column in the local newspaper.

10. Although making specific arrangements for your funeral may be discomforting, doing so will be a tremendous help to your family. It will ease the decision-making burden they will inevitably face. Any questions you have about the various possibilities may be discussed with the rabbi of your temple.

11. Laws regarding Living Will, Organ Donation, and Durable Power of Attorney may vary from location to location. It is prudent to check the laws for your specific jurisdiction.

12. Many airlines have an emergency bereavement fare that grants immediate family survivors an exemption from fare restrictions. Make certain that your loved ones are aware of this bereavement fare. They will be asked to supply the details of the death, the doctor and hospital location (if applicable) of the deceased, and the name of the funeral home.

Life Data

1. Name _____

   Hebrew Name _____

2. Legal Residence _____

   _____

3. Telephone Number _____

4. Birthplace and Date _____

5. Spouse or Next of Kin _____

6. Conversion: Date/Place/Under Auspices of _____

   _____

7. Children (Name and Social Security Numbers)

   _____

   _____

_____

_____

8. Parents: Mother (Maiden Name) _____

   Mother's Hebrew Name _____

   Father _____

   Father's Hebrew Name _____

9. Grandparents: Maternal_____

   Grandparents: Paternal _____

10. Grandchildren

_____

_____

_____

_____

11. Social Security Number _____

12. VA Claim Number _____

13. Service Serial Number _____

14. Date and Place of Discharge _____

15. Length of Residence in Present Location_____

16. Blood/Genetic Information _____

_____

_____

17. Citizenship Naturalization Information (if applicable) _____

_____

People to Notify Immediately After Death

1. Rabbi _____ Tel. No._____

2. Office, Partner, Staff

   _____ Tel. No._____

   _____ Tel. No._____

   _____ Tel. No._____

3. Funeral Director _____ Tel. No._____

   The funeral director's services include arranging for flowers, clothing for the deceased, transportation, funeral chapel, space rental, etc. Costs vary according to the location and what services are to be included. Federal law in the United States requires that costs for these services be itemized. In addition to taking care of the details of the funeral itself, many funeral directors can help the family in other ways, such as contacting fraternal or professional organizations, obtaining certified copies of the death certificate, and placing newspaper notices. Note: Check with the funeral director about VA and Social Security forms.

4. My body has been bequeathed to medical science   Yes_____ No_____

   Contact _____ Tel. No._____

5. Attorney _____ Tel. No._____

   The importance of securing good legal advice at this time cannot be overemphasized. The local Bar Association can recommend an attorney if there is no family lawyer. The attorney can give legal advice on matters such as trusts, recording deeds to real property, conservation and disbursement of estate assets, and revising or drawing up a will for the survivor. The executor of the estate probates the will with the legal advice of the attorney. If there is no will, the court will appoint an administrator for the estate. The executor and the attorney usually go to the probate court within one month of the person's death. Probate is a civil proceeding that establishes the will, marshaling and protecting the decedent's assets and settling the estate. Probate court jurisdiction is generally understood to include the power to establish a will and distribute all property in which the decedent had an interest. Establish the attorney's fees before the will is filed for probate. Many states in the United States have set maximum levels by statute. The following information is needed for probate:

(a) The decedent's full name, address, and date of death

(b) The names and addresses of all the decedent's heirs

(c) The will

(d) The nature and extent of the assets and debts of the estate

In addition, if you desire, you may direct your attorney to fill out your estate tax return and your inheritance tax return.

6. Accountant _____ Tel. No._____

Often the person's accountant or tax consultant can assist the survivor or the executor of the estate by preparing and interpreting financial records and providing tax information. The accountant or consultant may also prepare the estate and inheritance tax returns.

7. Executor/Executrix of Will

(1)_____ Tel. No._____

(2)_____ Tel. No._____

(3)_____ Tel. No._____

The responsibilities of the executor include:

(a) Probating the will with the attorney

(b) Collecting or settling the decedent's debts. Only the executor should become involved in this matter since only enforceable claims against the decedent are deductible from the gross estate

(c) Deciding upon the sale of estate property not held in joint tenancy

8. Life Insurance Agent_____ Tel. No._____

The life insurance agent should be notified promptly. It is important to note that life insurance benefits can be paid in a variety of ways. Most life insurance companies provide options whereby the money can be paid within various periods of time in various amounts. Unless there is an immediate need for all of the cash in a lump sum, the other settlement options should be considered. In order to gain time to adjust to a changed situation and avoid rushing into financial decisions, the survivor can tell the insurance company that he or she needs a certain amount of money for immediate funds and that the company should keep the rest of the benefits under the interest option until a later date. He or she should do this only with the understanding that any amount could be withdrawn at any time, that the interest would begin immediately, and that the right to select any settlement option is guaranteed, including a lump sum payment at a later date. Settlement options often vary and differ from company to company. The insurance agent should explain each option fully. Note: Please check other avenues of life insurance, i.e. credit cards (if in deceased's name) and pension plans.

9. Bank Trust Officer _____ Tel No. _____

A trust may have been arranged ahead of time with a bank trust officer. It is the trust officer's responsibility to review his or her client's entire financial picture (real estate, individually owned securities, cash, personal effects—including works of art, automobiles, jewelry, joint property—business interests, and the face value of life insurance). Trust officers invest funds, collect income earned by the investments, remit the income, and attend to all the details involved in handling the trust. They will keep the necessary financial records and provide the family with the required reports. If a trust has not been already established, the survivor can arrange for the establishment of a trust benefiting his or her children or a living trust for the survivor's own benefit. The creation of a living trust will enable the client to obtain the professional services of a trust administration officer. The fees charged for trust services are based on the administrative services performed by the trustee. They are competitively set and are listed in a schedule that is available from the bank.

10. Pallbearers

_____ Tel. No._____

_____ Tel. No._____

_____ Tel. No._____

_____ Tel. No._____

_____ Tel. No._____

_____ Tel. No._____

_____ Tel. No._____

_____ Tel. No._____

11. Honorary Pallbearers

_____ Tel. No._____

_____ Tel. No._____

_____ Tel. No._____

_____ Tel. No._____

12. Other Relatives and Close Friends

_____ Tel. No. _____

_____ Tel. No. _____

_____ Tel. No. _____

_____ Tel. No. _____

_____ Tel. No. _____

_____ Tel. No. _____

_____ Tel. No. _____

_____ Tel. No. _____

_____ Tel. No. _____

The rest of the family and friends are listed in the address book of the deceased, which can be found

_____

13. Human Resources/Benefits Contact

Important information may be obtained from these individuals regarding benefits due to family.

_____ Tel. No. _____

Instructions to the Rabbi

____Burial Service ____in the synagogue ____at the funeral home ____at the graveside

Following immediate cremation or gift of body to medical science

____Memorial Service   ____in the synagogue   ____at the funeral home

The committal should be   ____ public   ____private

Specific suggestions for the service, i.e., biblical readings, hymns, or music

_____

_____

_____

_____

____Flowers

____Memorial gifts to _____ temple fund

____Memorial gifts to other agencies or foundations

_____

_____

Other instructions or comments

_____

_____

_____

_____

_____

_____

_____

_____

Date _____ Signature _____

Instructions to the Funeral Director

1. I would

   (a) ____like to be buried

   (b) ____like to be cremated

2. I would

    (a) ____like the service held at the funeral home

    (b) ____like the service held at the temple

    (c) ____like to have only a graveside service

3. I would

    (a) ____like the service to be public

    (b) ____like the service to be private

4. I would

    (a) ____like flowers

    (b) ____not like flowers

5. I would like donations in my memory made to

_____

_____

6. I would

    (a) ____like to be buried in a shroud

    (b) ____like to be buried in street clothes, specifically_____

    (c) ____like to be buried in a kippah

    (d) ____like to be buried in a tallit

7. I would like to be buried with (jewelry, a favorite possession, soil from Israel, etc.)

_____

_____

8. I would

    (a) ____like my remains interred in a wooden casket

    (b ____ prefer other, specifically _____

9. Jewish tradition lays out guidelines for what a funeral service should include.

    Examples:

____no embalming/cremation

____all wooden casket (doweled/glued–no metal)

____shroud

____*shomer*–person to remain with body until the funeral

____*k'vurah*–covering grave by family and friends

____*k'riah*–rending mourner's clothing (symbolically tearing ribbon worn by mourner)

As part of your pre-need discussions with your rabbi and family, it will be important to check off those items that you feel are important to you.

10. Gravemarker

    (a) ____stone or ____bronze

    (b) ____decoration _____

    (c) ____inscription _____

11. Gravesite

    (a) family plot located _____

    (b) family tomb located _____

    (c) previously purchased gravesite located _____

_____

12. Other wishes

_____

_____

13. Give obituary to newspapers. Include the following text or details:

_____

_____

_____

_____

_____

_____

_____

_____

_____

_____

_____

_____

Views on Disposition of Property, Securities, Art, Income

_____

_____

_____

_____

_____

_____

_____

_____

_____

_____

_____

_____

Other Special Instructions

_____

_____

_____

_____

_____

_____

_____

_____

Note: Your views on disposition of property, securities, etc., as well as other special instructions are not legally binding unless contained in a validly executed Last Will and Testament.

Places of Safekeeping

1. Safe-Deposit Box(es) _____
                              (location and number of box)

   The box(es) may be opened by any signer who has a key. If there is no cosigner for the box(es), the executor of the estate will have to present Letters Testamentary (or Letters of Administration, if an administrator has been appointed) and the box(es) may be opened by the executor in the presence of an officer of the bank or the safe-deposit company. Check with the establishment to determine whether it is their policy to seal a safe-deposit box once the obituary notice has been published.

   Key(s) _____

2. Strongbox _____

   Key or combination _____

3. Home Safe _____

   Key or combination _____

4. Home Desk _____

   Key _____

5. Office Desk _____

   Key _____

6. Home Files _____

   Key _____

7. Office Files _____

   Key _____

8. Locker _____

   Key or combination _____

9. Briefcase _____

   Key or combination _____

10. Ministorage/Warehouse _____

    Key _____

Location of Tangible Property

1. Cash _____

   _____

2. Jewelry _____

   _____

3. Objects of Art _____

   _____

4. Furs (Storage?) _____

   _____

5. Boats, Aircraft, Motor Vehicles, etc. _____

   _____

6. Other_____

   _____

   _____

   _____

   _____

   _____

   _____

   _____

   _____

   _____

   _____

   _____

Location of Documents

1. Will _____

   The assets listed in numbers 2 to 4 are considered outside the jurisdiction of the probate court.

2. Life Insurance Policy (if payable to beneficiary other than the estate)

   _____

3. Jointly Owned Property

   Deed to Home_____

   Deeds to Other Property_____

   _____

4. Trusts _____

5. Stocks/Securities Certificates _____

_____

6. Bonds _____

_____

7. Real Property of the Deceased Not Held Jointly (must be probated)

_____

_____

_____

_____

_____

_____

8. Other Assets (i.e., royalties, patents, etc.)

_____

_____

_____

_____

9. Other Insurance Policies

Health _____

Disability _____

Home _____

Umbrella _____

Auto _____

10. Bankbooks

In certain jurisdictions a survivor may withdraw funds only from an account that has been set up with rights of survivorship.

Savings _____

Money Market(s) _____

_____

Checking _____

CD(s) _____

11. Record of IRA(s) _____

12. Debts/Monthly Obligations

Mortgage:_____Home_____

Office_____

Home Improvement Loan _____

Others _____

_____

_____

13. Income Tax Papers/1040 Returns _____

_____

14. Records of Purchase/Sale _____

_____

15. Business Agreement/Partnership Contracts _____

_____

16. Pension Information _____

_____

17. Military Discharge/VA Papers _____

_____

18. Credit Cards and Account Numbers _____

_____

19. Title to Automobiles and Auto Registrations _____

_____

20. Marriage Certificate _____

_____

21. Birth Certificate/Adoption Papers _____

_____

22. Naturalization Papers _____

23. Change of Name Papers _____

24. Previous Marriage Certificates _____

25. Divorce Papers _____

26. Birth Certificates of Children _____

_____

27. Other Important Documents (i.e., Ethical Will) _____

_____

_____

_____

_____

_____

_____

_____

_____

Additional Contacts to Be Made

These contacts should be made as soon as the bereaved is able to attend to business matters. Notification may be made by phone or in writing. Sample letters and advice are included.

1. Social Security   _____

   _____

   Social Security benefits are not automatic. One must apply for them. Providing the following information will speed the processing of a claim:

   (a) A certified copy of the death certificate

   (b) The decedent's Social Security number

   (c) A record of the decedent's earnings in the current and previous year

   (d) A copy of the marriage certificate and any prior divorce decrees for either the decedent or the survivor

   (e) Social Security numbers of the survivor and dependent children

   (f) Proof of the survivor's age and the ages of dependent children who are eighteen or younger

2. Veteran's Administration   _____

   _____

   Benefits vary according to the nature of the veteran's death. The Veteran's Administration will require the following documents in order to process a claim:

   (a) The veteran's Report of Separation from Active Service, Form DD214 (discharge papers)

   (b) A certified copy of the death certificate

   (c) A copy of the marriage certificate and any prior divorce decrees for either the veteran or the survivor

   (d) Copies of birth verification for dependent children

   In addition, the veteran's complete name and Government Life Insurance policy number or VA claim number should be supplied. If this information is not available, the military service serial number and branch, as well as the veteran's dates of service, must be provided. The Veteran's Administration representative can help obtain the necessary documents from the Department of Defense if they cannot be located.

3. Companies to Whom the Deceased Owed Money

   _____

_____

_____

Many types of installment purchases, loans, and credit accounts are covered by credit life insurance, which pays off the balance due in the event of death. It is possible that a credit card account, car, boat, or other financed purchase becomes fully paid when the purchaser dies. All such companies should be contacted.

4. Holder of Pension Plan _____

_____

5. Insurance Companies

All insurance policies should be transferred to the survivor as soon as possible to avoid any lapse in coverage.

Auto _____   Agent_____

Home _____   Agent_____

Health _____   Agent_____

A survivor and dependent children may continue to be eligible for hospital, surgical, and disability benefits under the decedent's policy. These coverages may or may not cease with the death of the policyholder. The health insurance company should be contacted.

Disability _____

Umbrella _____

6. Mortgage Company _____

7. County Tax Assessor-Collector: Concerning Auto Registration and Title Change

_____

8. Utility Companies

The name on all bills should be changed from that of the deceased.

(a) Gas _____

(b) Electric _____

(c) Water _____

(d) Telephone _____

9. Other Organizations

Contact any service organization, automobile club, fraternal organization, etc., to which the decedent belonged for information on possible benefits. Many organizations have group life insurance credit unions or will return unused annual dues.

_____

_____

_____

_____

_____

_____

_____

10. Bankers

_____

_____

_____

_____

_____

11. Brokers

_____

_____

_____

_____

_____

12. Other

_____

_____

_____

_____

_____

Sample Letters

1. Veteran's Administration

Dear Sir/Madam,

I understand that the funeral director has informed you that (full name of decedent) passed away on (day, month, year). I would like to schedule an appointment with your representative on (give a preferred date and time, morning or afternoon, and two alternative dates and times). The deceased's Government Life Insurance Policy number is _____; his/her VA "c" (claim) number is _____; his/her military service number is _____. He/She served in the U.S. (branch of service) from _____ to _____. Please inform me if you require any additional documents or information. My telephone number is (area code) _____.

Sincerely yours,

(Survivor's signature)

(Typed survivor's complete *given* name and accurate address)

2. Life Insurance Company

Dear Sir/Madam,

Please send me the necessary instructions and papers to complete a claim under policy number(s) _____ on the life of (full name of decedent) _____, who passed away on (day, month, year). I wish to exercise my right as beneficiary to elect settlement options. Please search your files for any other coverages that the deceased may have had.

Sincerely yours,

(Survivor's signature)

(Typed survivor's *given* name and accurate address)

3. Companies to Whom the Deceased Owed Money

Dear Sir/Madam,

This is to inform you that (full name of decedent) passed away on (day, month, year). I understand that his/her loan may be covered by a life insurance plan through your company. Please let me know.

> Sincerely yours,
>
> (Survivor's signature)
>
> (Typed survivor's complete *given* name and accurate address)

4. Organization of Which the Deceased Was a Member

Dear Sir/Madam,

This is to advise you that (full name of decedent) passed away on (day, month, year). I understand that he/she may have been covered by a life insurance plan through your organization. Please let me know what information you need from me as beneficiary.

> Sincerely yours,
>
> (Survivor's signature)
>
> (Typed survivor's complete *given* name and accurate address)

3

Frequently Asked Questions on Advance Directives for Health Care

Planning Ahead for Important Heath Care Decisions

From The New Jersey Commission On Legal and Ethical Problems in the Delivery of Health Care—A Legislative Study Commission, March 1991

Questions and Answers

Why should I consider writing an advance directive?

Serious injury, illness, or mental capacity may make it impossible for you to make health care decisions for yourself. In these situations, those legally responsible for your care will have to make decisions according to your wishes. Advance directives are legal documents that provide information about your treatment preferences to those caring for you, helping to insure that your wishes are respected even when you can't make decisions yourself. A clearly written directive helps prevent disagreements among those close to you and alleviates some of the burdens of decision making that are often experienced by family members, friends, and health care providers.

When does my advance directive take effect?

Your directive takes effect when you no longer have the ability to make decisions about your health care. This judgement is normally made by your attending physicians and by any additional physicians who may be required by law to examine you. If there is any doubt about your ability to make such decisions, your doctor will hopefully consult with another doctor who has training and experience in this area. Together they will decide if you are unable to make your own health care decision.

What happens if I regain the ability to make my own decisions?

If you regain the ability to make decisions, then you resume making your own decisions directly. Your directive is in effect only as long as you are unable to make your own decisions.

What is the advantage of having a health care representative? Isn't it enough to have an instruction directive?

Your doctor and other health care professionals are legally obligated to consider your expressed wishes as stated in your instruction directive or "living will." However, instances may occur in which medical circumstances arise or treatment are proposed that you may not have thought about when you wrote your directive. If this happens, your health care representative has the authority to participate in discussions with your health care providers and to make treatment decisions for you in accordance with what he or she knows of your wishes. Your health care representative will also be able to make decisions in accordance with your wishes and best interests as your medical condition changes.

If I decide to appoint a health care representative, whom should I trust with this task?

The person you choose to be your health care representative has the legal right to accept or to refuse medical treatment (including life-sustaining measures) on your behalf and to ensure that your wishes concerning your medical treatment are carried out. You should choose a person who knows you well and who is familiar with your feelings about different types of medical treatment and the conditions under which you would choose to accept or refuse either a specific treatment or all treatment.

A health care representative must understand that his or her responsibility is to implement your wishes even if your family members or others might disagree with them. Therefore, it is important to select someone in whose judgement you have confidence. People whom you might consider asking to be your health care representative include:

• A member of your family, a very close friend, or your rabbi

• A trusted health care provider. Please note, however, that your attending physician cannot serve as both your physician and your health care representative

Should I discuss my wishes with my health care representative and others?

Absolutely! Your health care representative is the person who speaks for you when you can't speak for yourself. It is very important that he or she has a clear sense of your feelings, attitudes, and health care preferences. You should also discuss your wishes with your physician, family members, and others who will be involved in caring for you.

Does my health care representative have the authority to make all health care decisions for me?

It is up to you to say what your health care representative can and cannot decide. You may wish to give him or her broad authority to make all treatment decisions, including the decision to forgo life-sustaining measures. On the other hand, you may wish to restrict his or her authority to specific treatments or circumstances. Your health care representative has to respect these limitations.

Is my doctor obligated to talk to my health care representative?

Yes. Your health care representative has the legal authority to make medical decisions on your behalf, in consultation with your doctor. Your doctor is legally obligated to consult with your chosen health care representative and to respect his or her decisions as if they were your decisions.

Is my health care representative the only person who can speak for me, or can other friends or family members participate in making treatment decisions?

It is generally a good idea for your health care representative to consult with your family members or others in making decisions, and if you wish you can direct that he or she do so. It should be understood by everyone, however, that your health care representative is the only person with the legal authority to make decisions about your health care.

If I want to give specific instructions about my medical care, what should I say?

If you have any special concerns about particular treatments, you should clearly express them in your directive. If you feel that certain medical conditions would lead you to decide to forgo all medical treatment—including life-sustaining measures—and accept an earlier death, you should clearly indicate this in your directive.

Are there particular treatments I should specifically mention in my directive?

It is a good idea to indicate your specific preferences regarding three kinds of life-sustaining measures: artificially provided fluids and nutrition and cardiopulmonary resuscitation and intubation. A clear statement about your preferences regarding these treatments will help avoid uncertainty, disagreements, or confusion about your wishes. The forms on pages 98–103 enable you to state specific directions about your wishes with respect to these two forms of treatment.

Can I request that all measures be taken to sustain my life?

Yes. You should make this choice clear in your advance directive. Remember, a directive can be used to request medical treatments as well as to refuse unwanted ones.

Does my doctor have to carry out my wishes as stated in my instruction directive?

If your treatment preferences are clear, your doctor is legally obligated to implement your wishes unless doing so would violate his or her conscience or accepted medical practice in light of your medical condition. If your doctor is unwilling to honor your wishes, he or she must assist in transferring you to the care of another doctor.

Can I make changes in my directive?

Yes. An advance directive can be updated or modified in whole or in part at any time by a legally competent individual. You should update your directive whenever you feel it no longer accurately reflects your wishes. It is a good idea to review your directive on a regular basis, perhaps every five years. Each time you review the directive, indicate the date on the form itself and have someone witness the changes you want. Remember to notify all those important to you of any changes you make.

Can I revoke my directive any time?

Yes. You can revoke your directive at any time regardless of your physical or mental condition. This can be done in writing, orally, or by any action that indicates you no longer want the directive to be in effect.

Who should have copies of my advance directive?

A copy should be given to the person(s) whom you have named as your health care representative(s), as well as to your family, your doctor, and others who are important to you. If you enter a hospital, nursing home, or hospice, a copy of your advance directive should be provided.

Can I be required to sign an advance directive?

No. An advance directive is not required for admission to a hospital, nursing home, or other health care facility. You cannot be refused admission to a hospital, nursing home, or other health care facility because you do not have an advance directive.

Can I be required to complete an advance directive as a condition for obtaining insurance coverage?

No. You cannot be required to complete an advance directive as a condition for obtaining a life or health insurance policy. In addition, having or not having an advance directive has no effect on your current health or life insurance coverage or health benefits.

Can I use my advance directive to make an organ donation upon my death?

Yes. Refer to the section on organ donation on page 105.

Will another state honor my advance directive?

It is likely that your advance directive will be honored in another state, but this is not guaranteed.

What if I already have a living will?

While you may want to review your existing living will or advance directive and make sure it reflects your wishes, there is no legal requirement that you do so.

Do I need an attorney or a doctor to write a living will?

You can consult anyone who you think can be helpful, but it is not necessary to do so. This booklet and the forms it includes are designed to enable you to complete your advance directive on your own.

Terms You Should Understand

Artificially provided fluids and nutrition: The provision of food and water to seriously ill patients who are unable or unwilling to eat. Depending on the method used—such as the insertion of a feeding tube or an intravenous line—and the condition of the patient, this procedure may involve minor surgery and continuous supervision by medical (and sometimes surgical) personnel and may result in injury, infection, and/or side effects.

Cardiopulmonary Resuscitation (CPR): A treatment administered by heath care professionals when a person's heartbeat and breathing stop. If administered properly and in a timely fashion, CPR may restore normal breathing. This procedure may include the use of mechanical devices and/or drugs.

Life-sustaining measures: Any medical procedure, device, artificially provided fluids and nutrition, drugs, surgery, or therapy that uses mechanical or other artificial means to sustain, restore, or supplant a vital bodily function, thereby prolonging the life of a patient.

Decision-making capacity: A patient's ability to understand the benefits and risks of a proposed medical treatment and its alternatives and to reach an informed decision.

Health care representative or Health Care Proxy: A person who has been legally designated to make decisions on an individual's behalf in the event that the individual loses the capacity to make decision. A health care representative is appointed through the execution of a proxy directive (a durable power of attorney for health care).

Terminal condition: The terminal stage of an irreversibly fatal illness, disease, or condition. While determination of a specific life expectancy is not required for a diagnosis of a terminal condition, a prognosis of a life expectancy of one year or less with or without treatment is generally considered terminal. In many situations, a six month period is used regarding hospice care.

Permanent unconsciousness: A medical condition defined as total and irreversible loss of consciousness. The term "permanently unconscious" includes the conditions of a persistent vegetative state and an irreversible coma. Patients in this condition cannot interact with their surroundings or other people and do not experience pleasure or pain.

Persistent vegetative state: A condition of permanent unconsciousness in which the patient loses all capacity for interaction with his or her environment or other people. This condition is usually caused by an injury to the brain. It is normally not regarded to be terminal. With the aid of medical care, artificial fluids, and nutrition, patients can survive for many years.

Incurable and irreversible chronic diseases: Disabling diseases such as ALS, Alzheimer's disease, organic brain syndrome, or other diseases that get progressively worse over time and eventually result in death. Depending on the disease, the patient may also experience partial or complete loss of physical and mental abilities. Because the rate at which these diseases advance may be slow, such diseases are not considered terminal in their early stages.

Whole brain death: Death as a result of total and irreversible loss of all functions of the entire brain, including the brain stem. The criteria of whole brain death must be used to determine death in individuals who have suffered massive or total brain damage but whose heart and lungs are kept functioning by machines. Brain-dead individuals are not vegetative or in a coma but are, in fact, dead, according to internationally accepted criteria and much of contemporary Judaism.

Attending physician: The doctor directly responsible for your medical treatment. He or she may or may not be your regular family physician. Depending on your health care needs, the attending physician may consult with others in order to diagnose and treat your medical condition, but he or she remains directly responsible for your care.

4

Matan Chaim:
The Gift of Life

Information on Organ Donation and Jewish Tradition

*Union of American Hebrew Congregations
Department of Jewish Family Concerns,
Bio-Ethics Program Guide, #9:
Organ Donation, Spring 1997*

The issue of organ donation and transplantation has recently occupied a larger role on the debates and discussions having to do with ethical decision making.

Gradually, more and more people began to ask as to how Judaism treated the issues of donation and transplantation. The continuing growth of medical technology allowed much of this discussion to take place with renewed interest and gave rise to the reality of a continuing evolving scholarly tradition which seems to continue to find ways to honor life.

At the foundation of *Matan Chaim* is the fundamental Jewish belief in life and the ultimate affirmation of the value of saving life. Within your congregation and community there are people who can give witness to the reality of organ donation and transplantation. The effect, on the donor family and the recipient, is literally life altering and filled with profound aspects of holiness. A recipient wrote of his experience for his synagogue bulletin. Part of what he wrote speaks to the transformative power of his experience: "In times of difficulty, one comes to understand the true meaning of caring, the importance of community of family and friends. Friday night services become a key respite from the stress and anxiety of day to day, and the conversations with friends, their concern and support, even if momentary, are of great comfort. The words and melodies of the prayers take on a new meaning, as I search for some understanding and hope for the future.

It has now been almost four months since my miracle happened. . .so far a successful transplant. It is time to think of others, and for me to thank my synagogue, faith, family and friends for the strength to deal with the prolonged time of need. My reading tells me that for a Jew, to save one person is to save the entire world. The waiting list for organ transplants grows every day, in large part due to the success of these procedures. Organ transplantation is far beyond the point of experimental surgery—the major problem is the shortage of donors. Although 99% of people when surveyed would want a transplant for themselves or a family member, the donation rate is much lower. . . ."

Curiously, there still exists within our Jewish community perceptions that Judaism does not embrace the concept of organ donation and transplantation. In fact, the denominations are together in affirming the need for our participation in what is really a modern mitzvah.

The mood of contemporary Judaism, across the denominational line, favors organ donation and transplantation. The basis for this belief is rooted in the value of saving a life (*pikuach nefesh*). Strengthened by developments in modern technology, the acceptance of organ donation and transplantation has been affirmed by modern Judaism.

There have been a variety of CCAR responsa dealing with many aspects of the donation issue. Indeed, they were an important foundation in the creation of the UAHC *Matan Chaim* project. The 1968 Freehof responsa "Surgical Transplants" sets the groundwork for subsequent CCAR deliberations and develops interesting and exciting interpretations that deal with deriving benefits from organs of the dead and the conflict between honoring the dead and the thrust to save a life.

This same discussion, enhanced by the progress of technology and informed by the heightened awareness of the issue, is witnessed in a recent report of the Committee on Jewish Law and Standards of the Rabbinical Assembly (Conservative Judaism). Rabbi Joseph H. Prouser developed a *t'shuvah* entitled: *"Chesed* or *Chiyuv?:* The Obligation to Preserve Life and the Question of Post-Mortem Organ Donation." Published in December of 1995, this document also traces the Jewish value and textual approach to our issue. It likewise concludes that organ donation becomes a modern mitzvah, bringing various types of healing to both donor family and recipient.

The issue of not burying the donated organs with the dead body (an often-heard concern and a popular misconception as to why Judaism would not favor donation) is discussed by Prouser in a note from the former Chief Rabbi of Israel, Isser Yehuda Unterman: "As to the question of burial, Rabbi Unterman discusses only the particular organs or tissue being transplanted. In this regard, he considers transplanted tissue to be restored to life and thus not requiring burial with the donor's remains."

Likewise, the overriding belief in the saving of life also drives the contemporary Orthodox community to support organ donation and transplantation. As you will see from the CCAR and Rabbinical Assembly pieces, texts underscore the saving of life as a basic theological foundation for the Orthodox community. These positions also reflect the growth of medical technology and the impact of that technology on Judaism's reinterpretation of the definition of death. The Rabbinical Council of America (Orthodox) approved organ donation to save a life in a landmark decision in 1991. The decision noted that ". . .no halachic barriers exist to donation of the deceased if they are harvested in accord with the highest standard of dignity and propriety. . . .Vital organs such as heart and liver may be donated after the patient has been declared dead by a competent neurologist based upon the clinical and/or radiological evidence. . . .Since organs that can be life saving may be donated, the family is urged to do so. When human life can be saved, it must be saved. . . .The halacha therefore looks with great favor on those who facilitate that procurement of life-saving organ donations."

Frequently Asked Questions

What does Reform Judaism say?

Reform Judaism has long been an advocate of organ donation. A 1968 Reform Responsum commented that the use of such body parts in order to heal or save life is in keeping with the mood of Jewish tradition and a positive act of holiness.

Do other movements within Judaism agree?

Yes. The value of *pikuach nefesh* (the saving of a life) underscores this belief within our entire community, regardless of denominational affiliation.

Doesn't Judaism require us to be buried with our bodies intact?

Judaism does draw a distinction in the area of organ donation and transplantation in order to save a life.

What parts of my body can be transplanted?

Heart, kidneys, lungs, liver, pancreas and small bowel, as well as bone, heart valves, veins, skin and cornea. Bone marrow can be done while still living.

What about age?

Donors can range in age from newborn to 80 years old.

Can there be a conflict between saving my life and recovering my organs?

No. Donation can be considered only after every measure has been taken to save the patient's life and death has been declared.

How do I become an organ donor?

The completion of the attached donor card will allow you to become an organ donor. The Uniform Anatomical Gift Act of 1969 (USA) gives you the right to sign such a card. Patients who receive organs are chosen based upon many factors and are matched via need through a computerized system. Organ donation in Canada is covered under the Canadian Human Tissue Gift Act (revised in 1990).

Donor Card

I _____

have spoken to my family about organ and tissue donation. The following people have witnessed my commitment to be donor:

_____

Witness

_____

Witness

I wish to donate the following:

☐ Any needed organs and tissues

☐ Only the following organs and tissues:

_____

_____

Donor Signature   Age   Date

_____

Next of Kin Contact

5

The Dignity and Sanctity of Life

A Guide to Making Sacred Decisions at the End of Life: An Approach from Jewish Texts

It takes three things to attain a sense of significant
Being: God, a soul, and a moment.
And the three are always here.
Just to be is a blessing, Just to live is holy.

ABRAHAM JOSHUA HESCHEL

One of the goals of *A Time To Prepare* is to serve as a vehicle for discussion, as well as study, on how Jewish tradition can help us prepare for life's end. Medical technology often challenges our concept of dignity and sanctity. We are called upon to make decisions about care and treatment that raise questions regarding our tradition's belief that we are created *b'tzelem Elohim* (in God's image). We are concerned about how and if our own wishes will be respected. Often a family will be asked to inform a physician about the desired intent and extent of treatment. As a result, the existence of a completed medical directive and Health Care Proxy assumes great importance.

Our textual tradition gives us the insight to construct a method of making sacred decisions at the end of life. Passages from Exodus provide us with interpretations that teach the importance of healing in light of illness (Exod. 15:26; Exod. 21:18,19). Leviticus 19:16 calls on us not to shirk our responsibilities to seek healing when we witness illness, and an interpretation by Maimonides of a text in Deuteronomy underscores that it is a mitzvah to try and restore lost health to someone who is ill. (Deut. 22:2) The mood of these and other Rabbinic texts underscores what can be called a fundamental ethic upon which decisions can be constructed: *the dignity and sanctity of human life and the preservation of that human life in dignity and sanctity.*

This fundamental ethic, or basic value in Judaism, serves as the foundation for a methodology of decision making. The difficulty in the application of this value to all cases is manifest by the presence in our culture of two "wild cards": autonomy and technology. These two realities flow as twin currents through the social fabric of our world. They impact the fundamental value by introducing shades of gray, reminding us that decisions at the end of life are often not between what is good or bad, but variations of those themes, reflected against the wishes of the individual and a family.

Autonomy presents the contemporary Jew with a great challenge. The individual, as *tzelem Elohim,* does not exist in a vacuum. By virtue of our being born, we exist in a fundamental relationship with God and are called upon to model that relationship with others in the world. The prayer book speaks to a theology that reminds the individual that the body and the soul spring from the mystery that is God. We are partners with God in this mind-body-soul dialectic. Traditional prayers acknowledge the miracles of daily life. They celebrate the ability of the body to function as a balanced network and recognize that should something occur that would impede this network, our bodies would suffer and that we would be unable to stand in life with God. Likewise, the tradition teaches that the soul that has been given to us by God will be taken at the time that God chooses. This fundamental relationship between us and God is underscored in the prayer's final words which remind us that we are to bless God "in whose hands are the souls of all the living and the spirits of all flesh." Judaism teaches that we are not free to do what we want, when we want. Autonomy has limits, and in situations regarding extraordinary medical treatment at life's end, these limits can create profound spiritual tension.

The "wild card" of personal autonomy has an ally in the continually evolving arena of medical technology. The progress being made in the diagnosis and treatment of illness has further added to the vagueness of the absolute application of the fundamental ethic by providing people with greater choices than in any time in history. In end-of-life situations, this is especially true. The same technology that helps to prolong life can also simply delay the inevitability of death. Issues such as "quality of life" now occupy substantial amounts of dialogue. Without proper guidance, discussion and preparation, confusion, doubt and guilt are often players in decision-making discussions. That is one reason why every major denomination in Judaism now affirms the need to discuss end-of-life situations in anticipation of need. The creation of a personal Advance Directive for Medical Care accompanied by a Durable Power of Attorney for Health Care has become a modern mitzvah. Medical technology has made these discussions a necessity. Too often individuals find themselves in situations where their wishes for treatment are not known. They exist in a coma, at the end of a prolonged siege of dementia or in a vegetative state. With no discussion before hand, physicians and family members are left with few answers to difficult questions. The challenge is, of course, how to have these discussions in light of the widely held cultural belief in personal autonomy. This is where significant conflict may occur. How can we understand the wishes of an individual in light of the guidelines of Jewish tradition? How can we balance the belief that "this is my life" against Jewish tradition's belief that life is a gift from God and that the end of life is in God's domain? This tension may be understood by looking at the mood of Jewish tradition, which reminds us that while the amount of life granted to us may be out of our control, what we do with that life, its quality or meaning, rests squarely within our hands.

This introduces us to the possibility of a third "wild card," one that is emerging with increasing regularity and one that needs to be part of the discussion of how we apply Judaism's fundamental ethic to a particular life situation. This third factor is the desire for spiritual significance—the search for one's own meaning and purpose. This new dynamic is a direct result of the longevity revolution. As we age, we renew our search for how our life can be lived to achieve meaning. Jewish tradition stresses this point. Life is to be lived, even to the last moments. In each moment there is opportunity to find and provide meaning, even as life winds down. The works of Abraham Joshua Heschel reinforce our continuing need to search for the mystery of our own meaning within our existence. A theme of Heschel's writings is that we human beings are creatures who are constantly in search of meaning, and this search is cemented in a partnership with God. "To the biblical mind man is not only a creature who is constantly in search of himself but also a creature God is constantly in search of. Man is a creature in search of meaning because there is a meaning in search of him, because there is God's beseeching question, 'Where art thou?'" (Heschel, 1959, 238–239).

Judaism reminds us that even at the end of life, there can be meaning and the opportunity for mitzvot. This gives even greater importance to the need for families to discuss the issue of how to approach, treat, and manage the decisions that arise as life ends. In spite of the belief in personal autonomy, there still exists the desire for life to have meaning; a desire made all the more urgent in light of the choices brought about by medical technology. The value of life's dignity and sanctity and the preservation of that life in dignity and sanctity still remain our foundation. Yet, given the "wild cards," how can we begin to apply this ethic? Is it absolute in every situation?

No, and this the gift of Jewish thought in the area of decision making at the end of life, for the application of the fundamental value depends on the context of the case before us. Each individual case is best judged on its own, based on the particular situation. Decisions regarding a person's quality of life are best left to that individual or to a duly appointed surrogate if the individual becomes unable to make his or her wishes known. Again we see the importance of creating opportunities for these discussions to take place, discussions that will lead to the creation of necessary Advance Directives for Medical Care.

The importance of examining the context of a particular situation is reinforced by the specific legal guidelines that may impact when and how decisions are made. These guidelines are based on specific categories drawn from Jewish textual tradition. It is safe to assert that with the dignity and sanctity of human life as our fundamental value, it is not permitted to actively end a human life. It is safe to assert that everything should be done to return a person to wholeness and life. Jewish tradition emphasizes this value when it reminds us that to save a human life *(pikuch nefesh)*, we are permitted to abrogate almost every Jewish law. Yet, there does exist a boundary, drawn from Jewish legal tradition, beyond which different approaches to treatment apply. Up until that boundary is reached, the mood of Judaism is to mandate that everything must be done in order to save a human life. Once, however, that boundary is crossed, a different mood exists. That boundary is called *goses*, and it refers to a patient who is moribund and whose death is imminent. Here the "wild card" of technology comes into play for, while tradition defined imminent as within three days, current technological prowess has rendered that definition moot. It is possible to prolong a moribund person via technology. The question then asserts itself as to whether you are prolonging a life or delaying the death. The *goses* is a person whose flame of life is flickering out, and while we may not be permitted to actively snuff out that flame, we are enjoined to do everything in our power to make sure that the flame flickers out in dignity and sanctity. For the *goses* all aggressive medical treatment options have been exhausted. An individual may be hooked up to many machines; debilitating therapies may have been tried; and in the worst-case scenarios, the patient may even be unconscious. Are we still commanded to pursue aggressive treatment in such cases? Judaism says no. When the end of life is clear, when the journey has been completed, when the flame is flickering out, we are under no obligation to prolong suffering or pain, because that only reduces the value of dignity and sanctity. Ongoing communication between family, patient, health care provider and rabbi is fundamentally important in determining when a person crosses this boundary. There are no set rules. There is no set standard. Each individual and case stands on its own.

Jewish tradition's position that there are times when it is permissible to allow the flame of life to flicker out is based on classic Jewish texts. Jewish life draws its vitality from the evolving analyses of texts, analyses that allow current issues to be viewed through an historic lense of faith and relationships. The text that informs much of this discussion centers on the death of the beloved Rabbi Judah HaNasi.

Rabbi Judah was in the last stages of life. His students gathered outside his house in Jerusalem and prayed that he might live. Judah's maidservant, seeing that these prayers were actually hindering the natural process of Judah's death from taking place, ran to the top of the house and threw down a large pottery jar. The crashing of the jar on the ground caused the prayers of the students to stop and at that instant, Rabbi Judah's soul departed (Babylonian Talmud, *K'tubot* 104a). Rabbi Judah, in other words, was definitely *goses*. Given those facts, it was permissible to seek relief and allow the flame of life to flicker out in dignity and sanctity. This story also opens us to a discussion of the role of prayer in the healing and caring process. Many scholars understand that, in certain contexts, it is permissible to pray that an individual be granted release from the pain and suffering associated with the final moments of life. Given the realities of medical care that presently exist, we need to be reminded that dignity, sanctity, and comfort are basic Jewish values which need to be a part of the decision-making process as the final moments of life unveil themselves.

Too often, as life ebbs, families are called upon to make a decision about a loved one's care. The textual tradition of Judaism reminds us that while we are not permitted to actively end a life, when the category of *goses* is operative, it is permissible to remove what may be impediments to the natural, dignified means of dying. Rabbi Judah's story has echoes in other texts as well. Rabbi Chananya ben Teradyon, as he was being martyred, allowed the removal of water-soaked tufts of wool which would have delayed the impact of the fires that were consuming him (Babylonian Talmud, *Avodah Zarah* 18a). The classic Jewish law code of the sixteenth century, the *Shulchan Aruch*, continues this discussion when it calls for the removal of anything which impedes the final process of death, using imagery such as the sounds of pounding or wood chopping (*Yoreh Deah* 339.1).

Keep in mind that Judaism is clear on its insistence that no one may actively end a life. The *goses* is considered a living person. Yet, many people are faced with agonizing decisions regarding end-of-life treatment that go beyond simply removing so called impediments. Can we find guidance in situations where someone is dealing with great pain and suffering? Here, as well, we see possibilities of action. Pain and suffering are not values that bring dignity to a person or enhance a person's sanctity. In cases such as this, the category of *goses* is critical. In such a situation, is it permissible to increase types of medication in order to relieve excruciating pain and suffering, even though this increased dosage may hasten the person's death? If it is our intent to relieve the pain and suffering of a dying person, then the answer is "yes." If it is our intent to end a life, to "put this person out of his or her misery," then the answer is a resounding "no." A discussion drawn from Reform Jewish sources on the issue of relieving pain in the final hours of a person's life concludes that: "We may take definite action to relieve pain, even if it is of some risk to the *chayei-sha-a*, the last hours. In fact, it is possible to reason as follows: It is true that the medicine to relieve his pain may weaken his heart, but does not the great pain itself weaken his heart? And: May it not be that relieving the pain may strengthen him more than the medicine might weaken him? At all events, it is a matter of judgement, and in general we may say that in order to relieve his pain, we may incur some risk as to his final hours" (Jacob, *American Reform Responsa*, 1983, 256–257). A discussion from the Orthodox point of view affirms the basic mood of Judaism regarding these "quality of life" issues in the contexts of decision making at the end of life: "Judaism is concerned about the quality of life, about the mitigation of pain and the cure of illness whenever possible. If no cure or remission can be achieved, nature may be allowed to take its course. To prolong life is a mitzvah, to prolong dying is not" (Tendler and Rosner, 1993). These situations reinforce the need for families to have the necessary conversations with each other so that decisions can be made with knowledge of an individual's wishes. During many of the discussions, the concern for an individual's quality of life is often raised. Here again, the concept of seeking to understand the context of an individual and a situation is helpful. Quality of life is, by definition, a very subjective issue. Decisions regarding a person's quality of life are best left to that individual or to a duly appointed surrogate if the individual is incompetent. The completion of appropriate documents in connection with honest family discussion can be seen as a modern-day mitzvah.

The emphasis on examining the context of an individual's medical situation in light of treatment decisions points to a way of looking at these considerations in a non-linear manner. The "wild cards" that impact our current society have allowed us the opportunity to see the end of life as a gradual unfolding of stages. Rabbi Elliot Dorff has been instrumental in helping to develop this point of view. Responding to the impact of medical technology and the need for people to seek more control over their treatment options, Dorff has re-introduced a classic Jewish term into the discussions of decisions at the end of life. Building on the work of Dr. David Sinclair, Dorff writes of the concept of *tereifah*, which he defines as someone who has been diagnosed with an irreversible, terminal illness. This is a person whom it would be permissible to not treat in an aggressive manner, given this specific context. The person who has become *tereifah* is really no longer a healthy person and evolves into the status of *goses* in the last days, hours, and moments of life. Dorff echoes other scholars when he reminds us that in these final stages of life, we are mandated not to prolong death. Rather, the intent of our actions needs to be, by appropriate palliative and comfort care, to sanctify and dignify life (Dorff, 1998).

This category represents a new stage in the process of dying. Many individuals now function in this category. They may be in this stage for a long time, given the reality of medical technology. In this category greater leeway is available for decision making that may, indeed, prolong life. Indeed, it is in this stage that often someone will opt for more aggressive treatments; or, say to their physician and family, "enough." Again, the value of open and honest discussion and the evaluation of the particular context in which the individual finds him or herself is of crucial importance. Few of these decisions are arrived at without great anxiety, fear, and doubt. These are profoundly spiritual moments in which, as Herschel reminds us, the relationship between man and God is present.

The fundamental value of Judaism, viewed against the context of a particular case, allows us to make informed Jewish choices. Choice, a basic component of Jewish thought, is the final aspect of this decision-making construct. In Deuteronomy we are reminded that we are, in our life, given choices all the time. They are choices between life and death, good and evil, the blessing and the curse. We are called upon to "choose life" (Deut. 30:19–20), so that those who follow us will be blessed. Often it is difficult to see how the decisions that people must make regarding end-of-life situations can be seen as a blessing. The texts, as we have seen, often remind us that there is no blessing in pain and suffering and that there actually may be times when prayers are said so that a person can be released from the final stages of life. Examining the context against the values of Jewish tradition can give us secure guidelines for making Jewish choices. The discussion with family, care-givers and clergy of these values in light of a particular context is the pathway for coming to a sense of wholeness in what is a difficult stage in a family's life.

It is this desire to provide opportunities for individuals and families to seek the sacred and to celebrate the mystery of life that we have developed *A Time To Prepare.*

The Ethical Will

6

For I have singled him out, that he may instruct his children and his household after him to keep the way of Adonai by doing what is just and right, in order that Adonai may bring about for Abraham what Adonai has promised him.

GENESIS 18:19

These words marked the beginning of the custom of one generation's leaving an ethical will for the next. For centuries parents have left a document for their children through which they bequeathed a spiritual, moral, and ethical legacy. In essence this document is just another way in which we transmit the fundamental values of life's dignity and sanctity and fulfill our responsibility to pass on these values to those we leave behind.

A personal ethical will is a gift that a parent gives his or her child. It is a testimony about living—a prescription based on one's own experiences for living a righteous life.

Albert Vorspan, former senior vice president of the Union of American Hebrew Congregations, once described the challenge of leaving behind an ethical will in the following way:

> What is the true legacy I can leave my own children?
>
> It is not stocks and bonds and notes and precious stones. It is not even such wisdom as I may have accumulated in my life. For what is man and what is life? I have lived and I will die, but the deepest mysteries of life will no doubt be as unclear to me at the end as at the beginning.
>
> Each of us is but a puff of smoke in eternity. What is immortal about us is that we are part of an undying Jewish people. The wisdom which has been distilled in 3,000 years of unique history is the greatest legacy a Jew can leave his children. For it is not economic wealth, but moral and spiritual treasure which I can pass on to my children as did my ancestors through one hundred and twelve generations, stretching back to the midsts of Sinai. What I owe them is a chance to grasp a faith to live by.
>
> *Jewish Values and Social Crisis* (New York: UAHC Press, 1968), p. 193

Jewish writings have provided us with numerous examples of the ethical will. From biblical to contemporary times, the spiritual heritage of our people has been transmitted in uniquely personal ways. Some of these examples appear in a section on ethical wills in *Gates of Mitzvah*, pp. 139–143, published by the Central Conference of American Rabbis. The classic book on the subject is titled *Hebrew Ethical Wills*, edited by Israel Abrahams. In the foreword to the revised edition, Judah Goldin writes about the meaning of the ethical will: "The Hebrew ethical will is not mere valediction but an audacious attempt at continuing speech from father in the grave to children in a reckless world. The teacher's absence is not the end of instruction. It was said a long time ago, When the dead are quoted, their lips move."

We can continue to teach by participating in this ancient mitzvah of leaving for our children an ethical will. It should be compiled with the same detailed thought and planning that we devote to creating a will that instructs about the distribution of our property and assets and conveys our wishes regarding medical treatment.

What instructions, reflections, and impressions do we wish to share with those we leave behind? Based on your experiences and your life, what values of faith and community, of love and life, can you share in order to benefit those who remain? What dreams remain unfulfilled? What advice needs to be shared? What promises need to be kept? What legacy for living can you impart?

In a world of increased complexity, we often search for lessons of truth to pass on to the next generation. Thus we have the ethical will. One of the most beautiful and simple examples of the ethical will comes from the Chasidic tradition and concerns the instruction given by Reb Zusya as he lay dying. It seems that the students of Reb Zusya came to pay one last visit when they heard that his death was imminent. They entered his room and found him trembling. "Why are you afraid?" they asked. "Have you not been in your life as righteous as Moses?" To which Reb Zusya replied, "When I stand before the throne of judgement, I will not be asked, 'Reb Zusya, why were you not like Moses?' I will be asked, 'Reb Zusya, why were you not like Zusya?'"

MY PERSONAL ETHICAL WILL

FROM _____

TO _____

_____

DATE_____

7

Prayers and Meditations on Saying Good-bye

A Suggested Ritual for Saying Good-bye

There may come a time when one of your loved ones is on the verge of death and you are alone together for a few moments. Such a situation may take place at home and the patient may be lucid. In many cases, however, the setting may be a hospital or another medical care facility and the patient may be unconscious. It is a mitzvah to be able to pray with your loved one and, in so doing, say good-bye. A suggested brief ritual that you may want to use in such a situation appears below. It is by no means authoritative. You are urged to be as personal as time and circumstance permit.

Confession by the Gravely Ill

(May be read in one's behalf)

אֱלֹהַי וֵאלֹהֵי אֲבוֹתַי וְאִמּוֹתַי My God and God of all who have gone before me, Author of life and death, I turn to You in trust. Although I pray for life and health, I know that I am mortal. If my life must soon come to an end, let me die, I pray, at peace. If only my hands were clean and my heart pure! I confess that I have committed sins and left much undone, yet I know also the good that I did or tried to do. May my acts of goodness give meaning to my life, and may my errors be forgiven. Protector of the bereaved and the helpless, watch over my loved ones. Into Your hand I commit my spirit. Redeem it, O God of mercy and truth.

(As the end approaches, the following is said with or for the dying person)

יְיָ מֶלֶךְ, יְיָ מָלָךְ, יְיָ יִמְלֹךְ לְעוֹלָם וָעֶד.

God reigns; God has reigned; God will reign for ever and ever.

בָּרוּךְ שֵׁם כְּבוֹד מַלְכוּתוֹ לְעוֹלָם וָעֶד.

Blessed be God's name whose glorious dominion is for ever and ever.

יְיָ הוּא הָאֱלֹהִים.

Adonai is God.

שְׁמַע יִשְׂרָאֵל: יְיָ אֱלֹהֵינוּ, יְיָ אֶחָד!

Hear, O Israel: *Adonai* is our God, *Adonai* is One.

(Those who are present)

שְׁמַע יִשְׂרָאֵל: יְיָ אֱלֹהֵינוּ, יְיָ אֶחָד!

Hear, O Israel, *Adonai* is our God, *Adonai* is One.

(After the moment of death)

יְיָ נָתַן וַיְיָ לָקָח.   יְהִי שֵׁם יְיָ מְבֹרָךְ.

God gave and God has taken away. Blessed be the name of God.

בָּרוּךְ דַּיַן הָאֱמֶת.

Blessed be the Judge of truth.

Meditations

For everything there is a season, and a time for every experience under heaven:
A time to be born, and a time to die;
A time to plant, and a time to uproot what is planted;
A time to kill, and a time to heal;
A time to tear down, and a time to build up;
A time to weep, and a time to laugh;
A time to grieve, and a time to dance;
A time to throw stones, and a time to gather stones;
A time to embrace, and a time to refrain from embracing;
A time to seek, and a time to lose;
A time to keep, and a time to discard;

A time to tear, and a time to sew;
A time to keep silent, and a time to speak.

ECCLESIASTES 3:1–7

What can we know of death, we who cannot understand life?

We study the seed and the cell, but the power deep within them will always elude us.

Though we cannot understand, we accept life as the gift of God. Yet death, life's twin, we face with fear.

But why be afraid? Death is a haven to the weary, a relief for the sorely afflicted.

We are safe in death as in life.

There is no pain in death. There is only pain of the living as they recall shared loves and as they themselves fear to die.

Calm us, O God, when we cry out in our fear and our grief. Turn us anew toward life. Awaken us to the warmth of human love that speaks to us of You.

We shall fear no evil as we affirm Your kingdom of life.

Gates of Prayer, Chaim Stern, ed. (New York: CCAR, 1975), p. 624

I have set the Eternal always before me. God is at my side. I shall not be moved. Therefore does my heart exult and my soul rejoice. My being is secure. For You will not abandon me to death nor let Your faithful ones see destruction. You show me the path of life. Your presence brings fullness of joy. Enduring happiness is Your gift.

שִׁוִּיתִי יְיָ לְנֶגְדִּי תָמִיד,
כִּי מִימִינִי בַּל־אֶמּוֹט. לָכֵן
שָׂמַח לִבִּי וַיָּגֶל כְּבוֹדִי, אַף־
בְּשָׂרִי יִשְׁכֹּן לָבֶטַח. כִּי
לֹא־תַעֲזֹב נַפְשִׁי לִשְׁאוֹל,
לֹא־תִתֵּן חֲסִידְךָ לִרְאוֹת
שָׁחַת.
תּוֹדִיעֵנִי אֹרַח חַיִּים,
שֹׂבַע שְׂמָחוֹת אֶת־פָּנֶיךָ,
נְעִמוֹת בִּימִינְךָ נֶצַח.

PSALMS 16:8–11

Birth is a beginning
And death a destination.
And life is a journey:
From childhood to maturity
And youth to age;
From innocence to awareness
And ignorance to knowing;
From foolishness to discretion
        And then, perhaps, to wisdom;
From weakness to strength
Or strength to weakness—
        And, often, back again;
From health to sickness
        And back, we pray, to health again;
From offense to forgiveness,
From loneliness to love,
From joy to gratitude,
From pain to compassion,
And grief to understanding—
        From fear to faith;
From defeat to defeat to defeat—
Until, looking backward or ahead,
We see that victory lies
Not at some high place along the way,
But in having made the journey, stage by stage,
        A sacred pilgrimage.
Birth is a beginning
And death a destination.
And life is a journey,
A sacred pilgrimage—
        To life everlasting.

Gates of Repentance, Chaim Stern, ed. (New York: CCAR, 1978), pp. 283–284

8

Representative Resolutions and Responsa from the Reform Movement Concerning End-of-Life Decisions

Health Care Decisions on Dying

Submitted by the Committee on
Bio-ethics and the Commission on Social Action
Adopted by the delegates to the
UAHC Biennial, Baltimore, Maryland, 1991

BACKGROUND: Jewish tradition affirms the sanctity of life and the precept that all must be done to preserve life. It also affirms that when there is no hope for a patient, impediments to death must not be created, and a patient must be allowed to die in dignity.

Recent medical developments now make it possible to prolong artificially the process of dying in those whose deaths would otherwise be imminent. These developments have kept many patients alive after they have become incompetent and are close to death or in a persistent vegetative state, with no chance of recovery. Often these patients had not expressed or had not had the opportunity to record their views of death and dying in an enforceable way.

The prolongation of life through artificial procedures takes an enormous toll upon the spiritual, emotional, and economic resources of the patients, their families, and their friends and can result in protracted litigation. Patients who have expressed their desire or refusal of such procedures to prolong their life have caused clergy, physicians, and other health care providers to experience a variety of irreconcilable or unresolvable moral and ethical conflicts.

In the 1990 landmark decision *Cruzan v. Director, Missouri Department of Health*, the United States Supreme Court affirmed the following: (1) a competent person has a right to refuse unwanted medical treatment; (2) that right survives incompetency, and (3) that right should be protected when a decision to refuse treatment is clearly expressed with specificity by a competent patient. The *Cruzan* decision underlines the importance of expressing and recording one's wishes before illness strikes to ensure that those wishes be honored, to give guidance to physicians, other health care providers, family, friends, and clergy, and to avoid the trauma that ensues when a patient's wishes are either unknown or not clearly recorded.

Therefore, the Union of American Hebrew Congregations resolves to:

1. Reaffirm in accordance with Reform tradition that each individual has the ethical, moral, and legal right to make his or her own health care decisions and that such right survives incompetency.

2. Develop and promote educational programs to inform each member of the existence of issues relating to death and dying.

3. Encourage members of our congregations to use Advance Health Care Directives and/or other legally acceptable and binding writings, such as living wills and durable health care powers of attorney, for the purpose of memorializing their respective decisions.

4. Promote and support the enactment of national and also state and provincial legislation, preferably of a uniform nature, designed to facilitate the decision-making process set forth above.

5. Call upon member congregations to support and join in these efforts.

Compassion and Comfort Care at the End of Life

A Resolution of the UAHC adopted at the
63rd Biennial Convention of the UAHC
in Atlanta, Georgia, December 1995

BACKGROUND: Because the synagogue is the focus of our communal life and the setting of our collective deliberation about life's most important events, we affirm the obligation of the synagogue community to educate its members regarding Judaism's belief in the dignity and sanctity of human life.

As the end of life approaches, the choices before us become difficult and troubling. Possibilities of survival engendered by medical technology may also unnaturally prolong the dying process. Our movement has already affirmed the right to refuse medical treatment that only prolongs the acts of dying, but it is clear that not all needs are met by withholding or withdrawing medical treatment at the end of life. There are those who, nearing the end of life's journey, would choose to live. We have yet to assert the obligations that our community has to those who cannot be cured of their disease but whose future promises nothing but pain and suffering. While we acknowledge that many would choose not to endure such a life, most such choices do not need to be made when adequate palliative care and support can be provided.

Guided by the mitzvah of *pikuach nefesh*, we must strive toward an achievable goal: to provide a quality of life that is at least tolerable for each one whose journey ends in pain and suffering. Our effort must ensure that only rarely will that choice be beyond human strength. We assert that most of the tragic choices to end life can be avoided through the combined efforts of caring doctors, clergy, providers, family, and community. By providing caring support for families and assisting in the development of hospices and similar environments where spiritual and physical needs are met, our congregations can help preserve the meaning and purpose of our lives as we approach the end of the journey.

THEREFORE: The Union of American Hebrew Congregations resolves to:

1. Address our society's needs to provide adequate comfort care at the end of life;

2. Develop and distribute more educational programmatic material regarding a liberal Jewish approach to end-of-life decisions;

3. Develop and distribute material that would raise awareness of the issues of pain and suffering and quality of life in order to enable sound decision making by all concerned;

4. Encourage the expansion of opportunities for rabbinic and cantorial students and cantors and rabbis in the field to participate in training programs designed to develop skills in end-of-life issues;

5. Call upon our congregations to develop connections with Jewish hospice programs in their communities and to explore their creation where they do not exist; and

6. Call upon the Committee on Bio-ethics to work with the Central Conference of American Rabbis Committee on Responsa to provide us with guidance with respect to physician-assisted death and active voluntary euthanasia.

Relieving Pain of a Dying Patient

Responsa by Dr. Solomon B. Freehof
from American Reform Responsa,
(New York: CCAR Press, Volume LXXXV, 1975), pp. 83–85

QUESTION: A dying patient is suffering great pain. There are medicines available which will relieve his agony. However, the physician says that the pain-relieving medicine might react on the weakened respiratory system of the patient and bring death sooner. May, then, such medicine be used for the alleviation of the patient's agony? Would it make a difference to our conclusion if the patient himself gave permission for the use of this pain-killing medicine? (Rabbi Sidney H. Brooks, Omaha, Nebraska)

ANSWER: Let us discuss the second question first, namely, what difference would it make if the patient himself gives permission for the use of this medicine, though he knows it may hasten his death? There have been some discussions in the law in recent years of the difference it would make if a dying patient gives certain permissions with regard to the handling of his body after death. For example, he might ask for certain parts of the usual funeral to be omitted; and some authorities say that he may permit autopsy. If I remember rightly, this permission was given by the late Rabbi Hillel Posek of Tel Aviv. But all these statements, giving the dying man the right to make such requests, deal with what should be done with his body after death, but not with any permission that he may give for hastening death. After all, for a man to ask that his life be ended sooner is the equivalent of his committing suicide (or asking someone else to shorten his life for him). Suicide is definitely forbidden by Jewish law.

However, we are dealing with a person who is in great physical agony. That fact makes an important difference. A person under great stress is no longer considered in Jewish law to be a free agent. He is, as the phrase has it, Anus, "under stress or compulsion." Such a person is forgiven the act of suicide, and the usual funeral rites—which generally are forbidden in the case of suicide—are permitted to the man whose suicide is under great stress. The classic example for this permissibility is King Saul on Mount Gilboa. His death (falling on his sword) and the forgiveness granted him gave rise to the classic phrase, in this case, "Anus keSha-ul." Thus, in many cases in the legal literature the person committing suicide was forgiven and given full religious rites after death, if in his last days he was under great stress. (See the various references given in Recent Reform Responsa, pages 114ff, especially the example of the boys and girls being taken captive to Rome who committed suicide (B. Gitten 57b); the responsum of Jacob Weil, 114; and that of Mordecai Benet, Parashat Mordechai, Yoreh de-a 25; and the other responsa given in Recent Reform Responsa.)

However, a caution must be observed here. The law does not mean that a person may ask for death if he is in agony, but it means that if in his agony he does so, it is pardonable. In other words, here we must apply the well-known principle in Jewish law, the distinction between Lechatechila, "doing an action to begin with," and Bedi-avad, "after the action is done." Thus, we do not say that Lechatechila it is permissible for a man to ask for death, but Bedi-avad, if under great stress he has done so, it is forgivable.

So far we have discussed the situation from the point of view of the action of the patient. Now we must consider the question from the point of view of the physician. Is a physician justified in administering a pain reliever to a dying patient in agony when the physician knows beforehand that the medicine will tend to weaken his heart and perhaps hasten his death?

Jewish traditional law absolutely forbids hastening the death of a dying patient. It requires meticulous care in the environs of a dying patient, not to do anything that might hasten his death. All these laws are codified in the *Schulchan Aruch, Yoreh De-a* 339. See the full discussion in *Modern Reform Responsa*, pp. 197ff. If, therefore, this were definitely a lethal medicine, the direct effect of which would be to put an end to the patient's life, the use of such medicine would be absolutely forbidden. But this medicine is neither immediately, nor intentionally, directly lethal; its prime purpose and main effect is the alleviation of pain. The harmful effect on the heart of the patient is only incidental to its purpose and is only a possible secondary reaction. The question, therefore, amounts to this: May we take that amount of risk to the patient's life in order to relieve the great agony which he is now suffering?

Interestingly enough, there is very little discussion in the classic legal literature, beginning with the Talmud, about the relief of pain. Most of the discussion deals with the theological question of why pain is sent to us and how we are to endure it and with our attitude to God because of it. As for the paucity of reference on the relief of pain—that can be understood because, after all, in those days they had very little knowledge of opiates or narcotics. However, the Talmud does mention one pain-killing medicine which could be used in the ceremony of piercing the ear of a slave (*Kiddushin* 21b). This is the basis of all modern legal discussion as to whether anesthetic may be used in circumcision (see *Current Reform Responsa*, pp. 102ff). It should be noted in that responsum that most of the scholars agree on the permissibility of the relief of pain, at least in that ceremony.

But in the case which we are discussing, it is more than a question of relieving pain of a wound or an operation. It is a question of relieving pain at the risk of shortening life. Now, granted that it is forbidden to take any steps that will definitely shorten the life of the patient (as mentioned heretofore)—may it not be permitted in the case of a dying patient to take some risk with its remaining hours or days, if the risk is taken for his benefit?

This question may be answered in the affirmative. The law in this regard is based upon the Talmud (*Avodah Zarah* 27a-b). There the question is whether we may make use of a Gentile physician (in that case, an idolater). What is involved is the enmity on the part of an idolater toward the Israelite, and the fact that the physician may—out of enmity—do harm to the patient. It makes a difference in the law whether the man is an amateur or a professional. The latter may generally always be employed. Also it makes a difference as to the present state of the patient's health, as follows: If the patient is dying anyhow, more risks may be taken for the chance of his possible benefit. The phrase used for these last dying hours is *chayei-sha-a,* and the general statement of the law is that we may risk these fragile closing hours and take a chance on a medicine that may benefit the patient (cf. *Shulchan Aruch, Yoreh de-a* 154). See *Modern Reform Responsa,* p. 199, and especially the classic responsum on this subject by Jacob Reisher of Metz, Shevut Ya-akov 111, 75. In other words, this is the case of a dying patient, and the law permits us in such a case to risk the *chayei-sha-a* for his potential benefit.

However, this does not quite solve the problem. The law permits these last hours on the chance of curing the patient. But may we conclude from that permission also the right to risk those last hours, not with the hope of curing the patient, but for the purpose of relieving him of pain? Interestingly enough, there is a precedent in Talmudic literature precisely on this question (see the references in *Modern Reform Responsa,* 197ff). The incident referred to is in Ketobot 104a. Rabbi Judah the Prince was dying in great agony. The rabbis surrounded his house in concerted prayer for his healing. But Rabbi Judah's servant (who is honored and praised in the Talmud) knew better than the Rabbis how much agony the Rabbi was suffering. She therefore disturbed their prayers in order that he might die and his agony end.

In other words, we may take definite action to relieve pain, even if it is of some risk to the *chayei-sha-a,* the last hours. In fact, it is possible to reason as follows: It is true that the medicine to relieve his pain may weaken his heart, but does not the great pain itself weaken his heart? And: May it not be that relieving the pain may strengthen him more than the medicine might weaken him? At all events, it is a matter of judgement, and in general we may say that in order to relieve his pain, we may incur some risk as to his final hours.

Quality of Life and Euthanasia

Reponsa by Walter Jacob
from Contemporary American Reform Responsa,
(New York: CCAR Press, 1987), #83

QUESTION: Does Jewish tradition recognize the "quality of life" as a factor in determining medical and general care to preserve and prolong life? I have four specific cases in mind. In the first the patient is in a coma, resides in a nursing home and has not recognized anyone for several years. In the second, the patient is in a nursing home completely paralyzed and can not speak or make his wishes known in any way. The third is a victim of a stroke, sees no hope for recovery or even major improvement, wishes to die and expresses this wish constantly to anyone who visits. The fourth is slowly dying of cancer, is in great pain and wants a prescription which will relieve her of pain but will probably also slightly hasten death. All of these patients are in their early eighties; none is receiving any unusual medical attention. Should we hope for a new medical discovery which will help them? (Rabbi R. H. Lehman, New York, NY)

ANSWER: The considerations which govern euthanasia have been discussed by the Committee in a recent responsa (W. Jacob ed., *American Reform Responsa*, #79, 1980). The conclusion of that responsum stated:

> We would not endorse any positive steps leading toward death. We would recommend pain-killing drugs which would ease the remaining days of a patient's life.

> We would reject any general endorsement of euthanasia, but where all 'independent life' has ceased and where the above-mentioned criteria of death have been met, further medical support systems need not be continued.

The question here goes somewhat further as we are not dealing with life threatening situations, but with the general question of prolonging life when its quality may be questionable. In none of these situations has any current extraordinary medical attention been provided. In two of the cases the cognitive and/or communicative ability seems to have ended. In the third is a strong wish for death. In the fourth, the primary concern is relief from pain. Let us look at each of these cases individually.

For the patient in a coma and the one completely paralyzed and unable to communicate, a segment of the brain which provides intelligence seems to be damaged beyond repair. Judaism does not define human life only in terms of mental activity. Every person has been created in the image of God (Gen. 1:26), and so even those individuals who may be defective, i.e. the retarded, the blind, the deaf, the mute, etc., their life is as precious as any other. It is necessary to guard their life and protect it just as any other human life. This is also true of an elderly individual who has now lost some of her mental ability or power of communication. In fact, we owe a special duty toward these individuals who are weak and more likely to be neglected by society just as to the orphan, the widow and the poor (Deut. 14.29, 27.13; Jer. 7.6; Is. 1.17; *Shab.* 133b; *Meg.* 31a; *San* 74a; *Yoma* 82b).

Let us return to the individual who seeks death and constantly reiterates his wish to die. Although some rabbinic authorities feel that neither an individual nor his family may pray for his death (Haim Palagi *Hiskei Lev*, Vol. 1, *Yoreh Deah* #50), most of our tradition would agree that a person may ask God to be relieved of suffering. The decision, of course, lies with God. A servant of Judah Hanasi prayed for his release *(Ket.* 104a). Other ancient authorities pointed to similar examples *(Ned.* 40a and Commentaries). We would, however, discourage the individual from such prayer and rather seek to encourage a different attitude toward life. The growing field of psychology for the aged has succeeded in developing a variety of techniques for dealing with such long term depression. We would encourage the family and the patient to utilize these methods or any other form of counseling and therapy available.

The individual who seeks relief from her pain should receive drugs which may help, even though they may slightly hasten death. As this is a very long term process, the drug cannot be seen as actually causing her death. Suffering itself has never been seen as an independent good by Judaism. Even criminals destined for execution were drugged to alleviate their suffering (*San.* 43a). Similarly the executioner of the martyr Hanina ben Teradyon was permitted by him to increase the temperature and remove wool sponges from his heart in order to made death a little easier, though Hanina was unwilling to pray for his own death as disciples suggested (*A. Z.* 18a). We would, therefore, see no objection to relieving the suffering of the woman who is dying from cancer and for whom the drugs are not life threatening.

It is clear that in each of these cases, and in others like them, we should do our best to enhance the quality of life and to use whatever means modern science has placed at our disposal for this purpose. We need not invoke "heroic" measures to prolong life, nor should we hesitate to alleviate pain, but we can also not utilize a "low quality" of life as an excuse for hastening death.

Drugs to Relieve Pain

*Responsa by Walter Jacob
from* Questions and Reform Jewish Answers:
New American Reform Responsa,
(New York: CCAR Press, 1992) #151

QUESTION: Does Jewish tradition set a limit to the use of drugs in order to alleviate pain? Frequently, physicians seem hesitant to prescribe drugs due to the fear of addiction or other reasons. What is our attitude toward pain and its alleviation? (Rena T. Hirsh, Santa Barbara CA)

ANSWER: Jewish tradition is not ascetic and does not endorse self affliction through pain. The only exception is Yom Kippur, along with some of the lesser fast days. On that day we are commanded to "afflict our souls," but that does not entail real suffering, only fasting and abstinence from sexual intercourse. Even fasting is not necessary for those who are physically impaired. We feel no necessity to renounce this world and its blessings and so need not afflict ourselves in order to attain salvation in the next world. This is in vivid contrast to some forms of Christianity.

It is true that rabbinic tradition has interpreted the suffering of the people of Israel and of individuals, as either Divine punishment or as a test (Job; B.B. 5a; *Shabbat* 55a, etc). However, none of these sources and many others, has anyone been asked to seek suffering, rather than try to avoid it. During illness we may use every medical means available to avoid pain (*Shulhan Arukh Yoreh Deah* 241.13 and commentaries).

There are enormous variations in the pain threshold of individuals. Many physicians refuse to consider this or do not appropriately deal with the entire issue of pain. Sometimes this is because specialists, who do not communicate with each other, are treating the patient; each is concerned with a specific organ or system and none is aware of the total effect on the patient. At other times, it is simply due to indifference and a lack of interest in the patient, possibly because the attending physician has never suffered any serious pain. There is certainly nothing within Jewish tradition which would restrain the treatment of pain. We would have a greater fear of continuous pain than addiction.

We must be equally concerned with pain of the terminally ill. There is a fine line of distinction between alleviating pain and prescribing a drug which may hasten death. When the pain is great the physician should alleviate the pain and not be overly concerned about the latter consequence, as death is certain in any case.

There is nothing within Jewish tradition that would keep pain relieving drugs from being given when medically indicated. We would hope that the patient be made as comfortable as possible and that this will help recovery or make the days of life easier.

August 1991

Living Will

Responsa by Walter Jacob
from Questions and Reform Jewish Answers:
New American Reform Responsa,
(New York: CCAR Press, 1992) #156

QUESTION: What is the Jewish attitude toward a "living will"? (Loren Roseman, Norcross GA)

ANSWER: The "living will" provides a legal method in some thirty-seven states for terminating life support systems in the case of individuals who are dying because of serious illness or accident. The pain of family members or friends in comas over long periods of time and in a "persistent vegetative state" while attached to life preserving machinery has led to the consideration of such documents. At that juncture often no one will agree on what should be done. In some occasions the courts have intervened; in others eventually a family member or physician intervenes, but at the risk of subsequent legal action.

Those who wish to spare their family from this agonizing decision may decide on a "living will," a form frequently used with a proxy designation statement that reads as follows:

Living Will Declaration

To My Family, Physician and Medical Facility

I,_____, being of sound mind, voluntarily make known my desire that my dying shall not be artificially prolonged under the following circumstances:

If I should have an injury, disease or illness regarded by my physician as incurable and terminal, and if my physician determines that the application of life-sustaining procedures would serve only to prolong artificially the dying process, I direct that such procedures be withheld or withdrawn and that I be permitted to die. I want treatment limited to those measures that will provide me with maximum comfort and freedom from pain. Should I become unable to participate in decisions with respect to my medical treatment, it is my intention that these directions be honored by my family and physicians(s) as a final expression of my legal right to refuse medical treatment, and I accept the consequences of this refusal.

Signed _____ Date _____

Witness _____

Witness _____

Designation Clause (optional*)

Should I become comatose, incompetent or otherwise mentally or physically incapable

of communication, I authorize_____

presently residing at _____
to make treatment decisions on my behalf in accordance with my Living Will Declaration and my understanding of Judaism. I have discussed my wishes concerning terminal care with this person, and I trust his/her judgment on my behalf.

Signed _____ Date _____

Witness _____ Witness _____

*If I have not designated a proxy as provided above, I understand that my Living Will Declaration shall nevertheless be given effect should the appropriate circumstances arise.

The various statutes specifically exclude chronic debilitating diseases such as Alzheimers which are not life threatening and attempt to deal with other problems as well.

This approach raises many questions about traditional and modern Jewish perceptions of life and death. Is this akin to suicide or euthanasia? Suicide has always been considered a major sin (A. Z.18a; *Semahot* 2.2; *Shulhan Arukh Yoreh Deah* 345.2) and even its contemplation was considered wrong. We have also felt that euthanasia is not consistent with our tradition (W. Jacob ed., *American Responsa* #78, 79). We may see from the arguments presented in these two responsa that nothing positive may be done to encourage death, however, the "Living Will" is not euthanasia, but an instrument of antidysthanonic. Our tradition has felt that a *goses* (dying person) should also not be kept from dying after all hope for recovery has passed, and so the *Sefer Hassidim* stated that if the steady rhythm of someone chopping wood kept a *goses* alive, the wood chopping should be stopped (#723; Isserles to *Shulhan Arukh Yoreh Deah* 339.1). Some rabbinic statements limit the definition of *goses* to persons who will not live for more than three days, however modern medical technology has made these limitations obsolete. Earlier Biblical statements clearly indicated that no positive acts to abbreviate life, even when there was no hope, were permitted (I Sam 31.1 ff; II Sam 1.5 ff). In a later age Solomon Eger indicated that medicine should also not be used to hinder a soul's departure (comment to *Shulhah Arukh Yoreh Deah* 339.1). We may then safely say that at the critical juncture of life when no hope for recovery exists the soul should be allowed to drift away peacefully. We have become even more sensitive to issues of euthanasia through our own experiences with the Holocaust.

Love of life in all its forms is very much part of our tradition. Even when conditions of life are rather doubtful and when there might be serious questions about the "quality of life" we cannot encourage euthanasia (W. Jacob *Contemporary American Reform Responsa* #83) nor can we make assumptions about "the quality of life."

The modern development of medicine has brought wonderful cures and provides additional years of life even to those in advanced years. On the other hand its technology may leave us in a permanent coma or a persistent vegetative state in which we are neither alive nor dead. Such individuals may be completely dependent upon life support machinery. While this is acceptable during periods of recovery, we fear a permanent coma when the mind has ceased to respond and a plateau of mere physical existence has been reached.

When the Harvard criteria of death have been satisfied, life support machinery may be removed. This state of "brain dead" has been defined by an ad hoc committee of the Harvard Medical School in 1968 (*Journal of the American Medical Association* Vol 205, pp 337 ff). It recommended three tests: (1) Lack of response to external stimuli or to internal need; (2) absence of movement and breathing as observed by physicians over a period of at least one hour; (3) absence of elicitable reflexes; and a fourth criterion to confirm the other three; (4) a flat or isoelectric electroencephalogram. The group also suggested that this examination be repeated after an interval of twenty-four hours. Several Orthodox authorities have accepted these criteria while others have rejected them. Moses Feinstein felt that they could be accepted along with shutting off the respirator briefly in order to see whether independent breathing was continuing *(Igrot Mosheh Yoreh Deah* #174). Moses Tendler has gone somewhat further and has accepted the Harvard criteria *(Journal of American Medical Association* Vol 238 #15 pp 165 ff). David Bleich (*Hapardes, Tevet* 5737) and Jacob Levy *(Hadarom Nisan* 5731 *Tishri* 5730; *Noam* 5.30) have vigorously rejected these criteria as they feel that life must have ceased entirely with the heart no longer functioning, a condition belatedly established by Hatam Sofer in the eighteenth century *(Responsa Hatam Sofer Yoreh Deah* #338). We can see that although the question has not been resolved by our Orthodox colleagues, some of them have certainly accepted the recommendations of the Harvard Medical School committee. We are satisfied that these criteria comply with our concern that life has ended. Therefore, when circulation and respiration only continue through mechanical means, as established by the above-mentioned tests, then the suffering of the patient and his/her family may be permitted to cease, as no "natural independent life" functions have been sustained. We would permit a physician in good conscience to cease treatment and to remove life giving support systems. The "persistent vegetative state" is more difficult as "brain death" has not yet been reached. Such an individual would be considered a *goses* who is considered to be a living human being in all respects *(Semahot* 1.1; *Yad Hil. Evel* 4.5; *Tur* and *Shulhan Arukh Yoreh Deah* 339.1 ff.). One may desecrate the Sabbath to help him according to Jacob Reischer *(Shevut Yaakov* 1: 13), though others *(Kenesset Hagadol)* disagreed.

The long discussions about a *goses* indicate that no positive actions to hasten death may be taken, so he/she is not to be moved or his/her eyes closed, etc. As stated above there is no prohibition against diminishing pain or increasing the person's comfort or initiating new treatment which will not change the condition of the patient. Under these circumstances a "Living Will" may be helpful although we realize that we know little of the "inner life" of people in this state; we do not wish to terminate what may still be significant to them.

It would be permissible according to this point of view to help and assist those who may need to make these kinds of judgments for us in the future through a "Living Will." This may be especially important if there is no one present who can be counted on to make an appropriate decision in keeping with our verbally expressed wishes. The document must be worded so that it deals with the "persistent vegetative state" without moving toward euthanasia. The document should be sufficiently recent to assure that it reflects the wishes of the patient.

All of us wish for a reasonable exit from this world and would also like to make that period as bearable as possible for ourselves and our surviving family. The positive outlook on life which governs Judaism prohibits any drastic steps toward death but it does not insist that life continue when the person is a *goses*. At that point a peaceful release is permitted. The "Living Will" provides one possibility; the appointment of a proxy provides another.

March 1989

On the Treatment of the Terminally Ill
5754.14

Responsa from Teshuvot for the Nineties:
Reform Judaism's Answers for Today's Dilemmas,
edited by W. Gunther Plaut and Mark Washofsky,
(New York: CCAR Press, 1997) pp. 337–363

She'elah

A Jewish couple is providing care to two relatives with end-stage neurological disease.

Naomi, the couple's 16-month-old daughter, has Canavan's Disease, a rare progressive brain disease similar to Tay-Sachs, though the potential exists for the child to survive into teenage. She recognizes her family, smiles and laughs, but she cannot roll over, grasp objects, or hold up her head. Her vision is worsening towards blindness. She is not gaining weight. Her parents are concerned for her "quality of life": how much discomfort and pain should she suffer, enduring the medical procedures that might be introduced, for the kind of future that she will inevitably have?

Esther is the husband's 95-year-old grandmother and a patient at a nursing home. She has had Alzheimer's Disease for over ten years. She can feed herself and roll over in bed but needs help with everything else. She does not recognize her family but smiles with some activities. Based upon her previously stated wishes, life-prolonging medical care will be withheld, including antibiotics, hospitalization, and tube feedings.

What approach to medical care is most appropriate for Naomi? Is it justifiable to treat her in the same manner as a 95-year-old with Alzheimer's and withhold life-prolonging measures? Does her current "happiness" mandate some or all efforts to extend her life as long as possible? Does her future quantity or quality of life justify painful medical interventions? What differentiates these two cases? (Rabbi Norman M. Cohen, Hopkins, MN)

Teshuvah

I. On Euthanasia and Assisted Suicide. It is undeniably difficult to speak to the situation that confronts these parents. We know that whatever counsel we can offer will be inadequate in the face of the heartbreak they endure as they watch their daughter's deterioration toward an early, inevitable death. Yet they ask us to explore the resources of the Jewish tradition and derive from them a response to her illness that is both compassionate and ethical: compassionate in that it spares her unnecessary pain, ethical in that it meets our moral duty toward a human life that is infinitely precious in God's sight. How might they best achieve both these goals, striking a proper balance between them?

The parents do not suggest euthanasia, or "mercy killing," as an option for either Naomi or Esther. For that reason alone, we might be justified in ignoring the subject altogether. Yet it cannot be ignored; the issue of euthanasia and assisted suicide has lately become a hotly-debated one within our culture. In particular, some prominent Reform rabbis have proposed that we rethink our long-standing opposition to euthanasia.[1] Therefore, though it is not directly relevant to this case, we believe it to be our responsibility to examine that question, if briefly, as an essential first step in the consideration of the broader question of the treatment of the terminally ill.

Jewish tradition, as is well known, prohibits suicide, if by "suicide" we mean a rational, premeditated act of self-killing.[2] The prohibition flows from the tradition's affirmation of the sanctity, the inviolability of human life. This affirmation, in turn, assumes the doctrine that life belongs to God, Who has the final say in its disposal.[3] This implies that the individual has no right of "ownership" over his/her life, no authority to bring that life to an illegitimately premature end. For this reason, the court may not execute a criminal on the strength of his own confession, "for the human life is not the property of man but of God . . . one's confession cannot be accepted with respect to a matter that does not lie within his power . . . (for) one is not entitled to commit suicide."[4] Similarly, Jewish law prohibits euthanasia, or mercy killing. Inasmuch as human life remains sacred and inviolable until the final moment of its existence, the sources uniformly reject any distinction in this regard between the dying person *(goses)* and any other. "The dying person is like a living person in all respects" (*Semachot* 1:1). Though he or she lies in a moribund state in which death is imminent,[5] a person is still a person, a human being created in the image of God. This life is to be treasured and protected; even though the prognosis is hopeless, he or she deserves all appropriate care. Just as the laws prohibiting work on Shabbat may be violated in order to save life (*Pikuach nefesh),* so do we violate them on behalf of the *goses.* We set aside the Shabbat in order to treat this person, despite the fact that this is a life we cannot "save."[6] The one who kills the *goses* is guilty of murder.[7] The dying person is compared to a flickering flame: the slightest touch will extinguish his life. It is forbidden to take any action that hastens the death of the *goses,* "whoever touches him commits bloodshed,"[8] even though this act is taken out of compassion, in order to relieve him of terrible pain and suffering. If such is the case with the *goses,* then it is surely so concerning patients such as Naomi and Esther who, though incurably ill, have not yet reached the very end of life.[9]

On the other hand, the prohibition against suicide is not absolute. One major exception to the rule is the case of martyrdom: a Jew is obligated to accept death rather than to transgress the Toraitic commandments against murder, idolatry, and sexual immorality. Thus does one fulfill the commandment *of kiddush hashem,* of sanctifying the Divine Name through one's decision to die.[10] Some suggest that this requirement extends to active suicide: one who fears that the persecutors will, through excruciating torture, coerce him into violating the Torah may take his life in order to avoid committing that act.[11] Of special interest to our question is the fact that the sources look with considerable understanding upon individuals who commit suicide in extreme straits. A classic case is that of King Saul, who falls upon his sword rather than suffer a degrading death at the hands of the enemy (I Samuel 31:4). Saul, writes one commentator, "committed no sin in taking his own life" under these circumstances.[12] Some authorities derive from Saul's example that, while such an act is not "permitted," one who takes his or her life out of a desire to escape terrible pain and degradation *('oni uvizayon)* is not in fact a "suicide." Such a person has in effect been coerced by overpowering circumstances into this most extreme measure; that action is not the "rational, premeditated act of self-killing" forbidden by halachah.[13] This judgment coheres with the rabbinic tendency to exploit every available pretext in order to declare that a person, though he has died at his own hand, may receive all the customary rites of mourning normally denied to the suicide: "It is most unlikely that a person of sound mind would take such a horrible step."[14]

If the tradition responds with compassion and empathy to those who commit suicide, some contemporary observers go farther. Citing as a proof text the story of the death of Saul, as well as the talmudic narratives surrounding the deaths of Rabbi Chanina ben Teradyon and Rabbi Yehudah Hanasi, they argue that Judaism actually permits suicide and mercy killing for those who face the pain and agony of terminal illness. In doing so, however, the Rabbis face an interesting problem in interpretation. On the one hand, it is certainly true that these stories might plausibly be read so as to support the option of active euthanasia. On the other hand, through the long history of the Jewish study of the Bible and the Talmud, the texts in question have not been understood in this way (see Excursus). This is a point of no little importance to our discussion. We wish to know, after all, whether the "Jewish tradition" offers evidence in support of active euthanasia. It is for this reason that advocates of mercy killing cite these stories in the first place. Yet we find that the very *tradition* of learning which created these passages and which has studied them for fifteen centuries and more as sources of moral meaning declares consistently and unequivocally *against* euthanasia. Indeed, the message which emerges from traditional halachic thought on this subject is quite clear and uniform: we do almost anything to relieve the suffering of the terminally-ill, but we do not kill them and we do not help them kill themselves. It is always possible to read these texts differently than they have ever been read by the Jewish religious community, to discover in them levels of meaning that generations of rabbis and *talmidey chachamim* may have missed. Still, the unequivocal voice of the halachic literature renders it is most difficult to sustain an argument, based upon the citation of a few stories from the Bible and the Talmud, that the "Jewish tradition" permits euthanasia.[15]

As Reform Jews, of course, we consider ourselves free to ascribe "new" Jewish meanings to our texts, to depart from tradition when we think it necessary to secure an essential religious or moral value. In this case, though, we fail to see why we should do so.[16] We see no good reason, first of all, to, abandon the traditional Jewish teaching concerning the inestimable value of human life. If the doctrine of life's essential holiness means anything at all, it means that we must stand in reverence before the very fact of life, the gift of God that renders us human. And this reverence does not diminish as human strength declines, for the dying person still possesses life, a life stamped indelibly with the image of God until the moment of death. It is an awesome and awful responsibility we take upon ourselves when we determine to kill a human being, even when our intentions are good and merciful. Such an action is the ultimate arrogance, for it declares that we are masters over the one thing—life itself—that our faith has always taught must be protected against our all-too-human tendency to manipulate, to mutilate, and to destroy.

Second, we do not believe that the existence of pain and suffering constitutes a sufficient Jewish justification for killing a human being in the name of compassion. It is true that none of us wants to endure a state of physical or psychological agony, and none of us wants this for our loved ones. We have every right to administer treatment to relieve pain. In addition, we are under no obligation to take every conceivable measure to prolong a life of suffering; on all this, see below. It remains a fact, however, that pain and suffering are part and parcel of the human condition. We do not cease to be human, that is, when we experience suffering, even that of a terminal illness. The choice we face when we are ill is essentially the same choice we confront at every other moment of our lives: to determine what we, human beings in covenant with God, propose to do with the time and the strength available to us on this earth. All of life, its end no less than its beginning and its middle, is the arena in which we act out our humanity. Judaism, for its part, bids us to respond to the challenges of life by *choosing* life, to praise God whether that life brings us joy or sorrow.[17] Even in debilitating illness, when our freedom of action is severely limited, we yet sanctify the divine name by *living* our relationship with God, by striving toward nobility of conduct and of purpose, by confronting our suffering with courage. To say this is not to ignore the agony of the dying but to recognize a fundamental truth: that even when we are dying we have the power to choose how we shall live. We can kill ourselves, thereby accepting the counsel of despair, or we can choose life, declaring through our actions that despite everything life—all of it—is blessed with the promise of ultimate meaning and fulfillment.

Third, we are uncomfortable with arguments for assisted suicide that proceed from judgments concerning the "quality of life." While this standard may be persuasive to many, the quality of life by its nature is virtually impossible to determine. That is to say, the decision that "my life is no longer worth living" is an inescapably subjective one; it cannot be quantified, verified, or tested against any principle other than the conviction that one's suffering is no longer tolerable. For example, it is often suggested that the life of a patient in a protracted coma or persistent vegetative state lacks a minimal element of "quality" and that the patient is therefore justified in giving advance authorization for his or her euthanized death. Yet there is nothing inherent in such a condition that demands suicide or euthanasia; the sole "objective" warrant for mercy killing in this instance is the patient's stated desire to die. If so, on what grounds can we deny the "right to suicide" to other persons who state that desire, to persons who are paralyzed, severely depressed, aged and infirm? Are they not entitled to decide that their lives lack "quality"? Once we have adopted "quality of life" as our standard, we have no principled reason to oppose the suicide of *any* person (with the possible exception of children and the insane, who by definition cannot make a "responsible" choice), no matter how flimsy the justification, whether undertaken in response to terminal illness, or to chronic illness, or to psychological or emotional distress. So long as a person concludes that "I do not want to live like this," we would have no right to oppose that decision.

Indeed, what of persons such as the psychotic, the senile, the defective newborn, who have not made or cannot make their own decisions but about whom we can say with confidence that "no one should have to live like this"? Shall we declare for involuntary euthanasia on their behalf, in service of their "human dignity"? The experience of the Netherlands in this regard is both instructive and frightening. In that country, where euthanasia and physician-assisted suicide are officially tolerated, government figures record at least 1000 cases annually of active involuntary euthanasia, defined as "deliberate action to terminate life without the patient's consent." Private observers believe that the real figure is much higher, that it should include the approximately 5000 persons killed per year by lethal dose of morphine but whose deaths are currently classified as "pain relief." All this has occurred despite the fact that euthanasia in Holland is supposed to be "voluntary," authorized by the patient. In its study of the Dutch experience, the Board of

Trustees of the American Medical Association warns that such non-observance of the rules is inevitable once physicians, the guardians of life, become dispensers of death. Predicting similar (and worse) numbers should these practices become legal in the United States, the Board warns that "meaningful control by a society of (the practice of euthanasia) is illusionary once the physician-patient relationship has been so changed that death becomes an accepted prescription for pain and suffering."[18] Indeed, the move from voluntary to involuntary euthanasia is a natural one; for once we have convinced ourselves that the absence of an identifiable standard of quality of life justifies the destruction of that life, why should we hold ourselves back from acting upon our belief?

Our duty to the sick is to heal them or, when this is no longer possible, to care for them; it is not to kill them. The sick, the terminally ill, have a right to expect compassion from us, for such flows from the respect we ought to display to ourselves and to others as children of God. But they are not entitled to ask that we take their lives, and should they make that request, we are not entitled to grant it. For when we define "compassion" so as to include the killing of human beings, we have transgressed the most elemental of Jewish moral standards and the most basic teachings of Jewish tradition as we understand it. We believe that compassion toward the dying is a moral responsibility. But we also believe that this responsibility can and must be discharged without resort to assisted suicide and active euthanasia.

II. The Cessation of Medical Treatment for Terminal Patients. Jewish tradition teaches that we achieve this compassion through two means: measures aimed at the relief of pain, and the cessation of unnecessary medical treatment for the terminally ill. For example, the same tradition which rejects suicide and euthanasia also bids us to strive to alleviate the suffering of the sick and the dying. Patients may undergo risky surgery to relieve pain, even though the surgery may hasten their death; such surgery is, after all, legitimate medicine.[19] Physicians may administer powerful anti-pain medications such as morphine to dying patients, even though such a course of treatment may shorten the parent's lives, for pain itself is a disease and its relief is a proper medical objective.[20]

In addition to permitting such active measures, the halachah also supports the withdrawal of medical treatment under some circumstances from terminal patients. The classic source for the discussion of this issue is the comment of R. Moshe Isserles in *Shulchan Aruch Yoreh Deah* 339:1. Drawing upon material from the 13th-century *Sefer Chasidim*,[21] Isserles rules that while it is forbidden to take any measure that would hasten the death of the *goses* (e.g., by moving him or by moving the pillow or mattress from beneath him), "if there exists any factor which prevents the soul from departing, such as the sound of a woodcutter near the house or salt on the patient's tongue . . . it is permitted to remove that factor. This is not considered a positive act *(ma'aseh)* but merely the removal of an impediment." While the realia mentioned in this passage hardly resemble what we recognize as science, Isserles and *Sefer Chasidim* deal here with an issue familiar to all students of contemporary medical ethics. They distinguish between "active euthanasia," defined as the application of any factor such as physical contact which would hasten the patients' death, and "letting nature take its course," the removal of any existing factor which serves only to impede the patient's otherwise imminent death. The former is forbidden; the later is permitted. Should we draw the analogy between the technologies of the Middle Ages—the birdfeathers, woodcutters, and salt—and those of our own day, we would discover traditional support for the discontinuation of medical treatment ("turning off the machines") when that treatment can be viewed as "useless," an impediment to death.

A problem with this analogy is that the line which separates active euthanasia from the removal of an impediment to death is not always clear. Indeed, Isserles apparently contradicts himself on this point. On the one hand, he forbids the removal of the mattress from beneath the patient, an action taken on the grounds that "some people say that certain birdfeathers have the property of delaying a patient's death," because to do so involves physical contact with the patient which hastens his death. On the other hand, he allows the removal of salt from the tongue, which also involves physical contact with the patient and thus presumably hastens his death, because this is merely the "removal of an impediment." What is the difference between the two? Why may we remove the salt but not the mattress? Halachic authorities have addressed this contradiction in various ways. Some, opting for extreme caution, declare Isserles wrong and prohibit the removal of the salt altogether.[22] Others allow the removal of the salt as but an "insignificant" contact with the patient.[23] A third approach is provided by R. Yehoshua Boaz b. Baruch, the 16th-century author of the *Shiltey Giborim* commentary to Alfasi.[24] He notes that while it is forbidden to hasten the death of the *goses* it is likewise forbidden to take any action that unnecessarily impedes it.[25] Salt, which cannot bring healing but only impede the patient's death, should never have been put on his tongue. Whoever put it there has acted improperly; thus, its removal, even though it involves physical contact, is permitted as the restoration of the correct *status quo ante*.

The advantage of the *Shiltey Giborim's* analysis is that it turns our attention away from blurry distinctions between "active" and "passive" measures and toward the nature and purpose of those actions. The essential issue is the medical efficacy of the factor we seek to remove. Certain measures must never be applied to the *goses* because they lack any trace of therapeutic value. Offering no hope of cure or successful treatment, they serve only to delay his or her otherwise imminent death. Since it is forbidden to do this, to unnecessarily prolong the death of the dying person, these measure may be discontinued even if we must touch the patient's body in order to do so.[26]

This theory helps to translate the medieval language of the texts into a usable contemporary vernacular. Does there not come a point in a patient's condition when, despite their obvious life-saving powers, the sophisticated technologies of modern medicine—the mechanical respirator, for example, or the heart-lung machine—become nothing more than mere "salt on the tongue," mechanisms which maintain the patient's vital signs long after all hope of recovery has vanished? Answering "yes" to this question, some contemporary *poskim* allow the respirator to be disconnected when a patient is clearly and irrevocably unable to sustain independent heartbeat and respiration. Even though the machine is considered part of routine medical therapy (for patients are as a matter of course connected to it during emergency-room and surgical procedures), it has at this juncture ceased to serve any therapeutic function. They can no longer aid in the preservation or prolongation of life.[27] Once their therapeutic function is exhausted, the machines "merely prolong in an artificial way the process of dying. We must disconnect the patient from the machines, leaving him in his natural state until the soul departs."[28]

III. The Duty to Heal. Other authorities, it is true, reject the comparison of modern medical technologies to those mentioned by Isserles. Birdfeathers, woodchoppers, and salt on the tongue fall into the category of *segulah*, something mystical or metaphysical in nature, whose properties are not subject to scientific verification.[29] Moreover, even if we accept the designation of the respirator and other end-stage technologies and therapies as "impediments to death," Isserles describes a situation at the last moments of life, a point at which we are certain that "the soul is struggling to depart the body," when death is imminent and would occur almost instantaneously should the impediment be removed.[30] Even if it is possible to determine precisely when a patient has reached this final extremity (and we are well aware that medicine is not precise in this respect), the patients who concern us here clearly have *not* reached it. A *goses*, particularly one at the very last instant of life, is not the same as a terminally-ill patient, who may have weeks, months, or even years to live. Neither Naomi nor Esther is a *goseset*. The medical treatments they are receiving are, to be sure, keeping them alive, but since neither lies at the very doorstep of death, these treatments do not qualify as "impediments" to imminent death as the tradition understands that concept. If we view their situation according to the criteria of Yore De'ah 339, therefore, we must conclude that we are not justified in withholding these treatments.

Jewish tradition, however, offers another conceptual framework for thinking about the terminally-ill patient whose death is not yet imminent. Under this framework, we consider not only the patient's specific prognosis but also (and primarily) the nature of the practice of medicine itself. The questions addressed are: what is the Toraitic source of the commandment to heal? How does Jewish law understand "medicine" as an ethical obligation? And, most importantly for our case, does the obligation to provide medical care change or cease altogether when the patient's illness enters a terminal stage and when hope for successful treatment has vanished? Should the answer to this latter question be "yes," it might follow that some types of medical care may be withdrawn from a patient even before he or she has arrived at the very last moments of life.

The commandment to heal the sick is never stated explicitly in the Torah and is addressed but obliquely in rabbinic literature. A midrash on Exodus 21:19, which speaks of the tort-feasor's obligation to pay the medical expenses for the person whom he has injured, declares that "from here we derive that a physician has permission *(reshut)* to practice medicine."[31] It is Nachmanides who raises this *"reshut,"* a term that implies a voluntary act, to the level of a mitzvah, a religious and moral obligation. He bases this deduction upon a logical inference: since we rely upon the physician's diagnosis to determine whether and when to set aside the laws of Shabbat and Yom Kippur on behalf of the sick, it is obvious that medicine is an integral part of the commandment to save life *(pikuach nefesh).*[32] Maimonides, on the other hand, also believes that medicine is a mitzvah, but he derives the commandment from Deuteronomy 22:2, a verse which, according to the Talmud, imposes upon us a positive duty to rescue a person from mortal danger.[33] Both approaches see the obligation to practice medicine as a subset of the more general commandment to save life. It follows that the obligation to heal should be understood according to the definition of that more general mitzvah. And, say the rabbis, fundamental to that definition is the element of *ability.* That is to say, one is required to take action to save life (and, conversely, one is liable if one does not take such action) only when the action has a reasonable chance of success. Thus, as Maimonides puts it, "whoever is able to save another *(kol hayachol lehatzil)* and does not do so has violated the commandment: You shall not stand idly by the blood of your neighbor."[34] One is under no obligation to undertake useless actions, actions which clearly do not contribute to the rescue of another person, for such measures are not to be defined as "the saving of human life."

The same principle would apply to the practice of medicine: As with lifesaving in general, the obligation to practice medicine holds only when "one sees another in danger and one is able to save that person *(veyachol lehatzilo)"* by medical means.[35] Put differently, the point and the essence of medicine is to heal. It is for this reason, and only for this reason, that we are permitted to administer harsh drugs and invasive surgical procedures which, under non-therapeutic conditions, would be strictly prohibited as *chabalah,* the causing of unnecessary physical harm to the human body.[36] This would imply that once a medical treatment ceases to be effective and beneficial it ceases to be "medicine" as that practice is conceived by Jewish tradition. A physician is obligated to administer those measures which in the judgment of the profession are therapeutic: *i.e.,* they are regarded in medical opinion as contributing to the successful treatment of the disease. On the other hand, treatments which do not effect "healing" are not *medicine* and thus are not required. While we may be entitled to administer such treatments we are not commanded to do so, inasmuch as they do not partake in the saving of life.

This distinction is of great practical significance in the halachic discussion of some familiar problems of medical ethics. As we have seen, halachists rule that a terminally-ill patient may be given powerful pain-killing medications such as morphine, even though these drugs may actually hasten the patient's death, because the treatment of pain is a legitimate goal of medical practice.[37] Then there is the question whether a person has the right to refuse medical treatment. On the one hand, since medicine is viewed as a mitzvah and suicide is prohibited, it stands to reason that a person is obligated to accept medical treatment for illness. One leading authority deals with the case of an individual who refuses treatment on the apparently admirable ground that the preparation of the medicine would involve a violation of the laws of Shabbat. Such a person, he responds, "is a pious fool (chasid shoteh). This is not an act of piety but of suicide. He is therefore compelled to do what the physicians prescribe,"[38] that is, to accept proper therapeutic treatment for disease is an act of pikuach nefesh; it is a commandment, to which one has no right to say "no." This standard would apply, however, only to medical procedures classified as refu'ah vada'it or bedukah, tested and proven remedies which offer a reasonably certain prospect of successful treatment. On the other hand should a particular remedy be experimental in nature, if its therapeutic effect upon the disease is uncertain at best, then the patient is not required to accept it.[39] Under such circumstances, the treatment is no longer classified as "life-saving" and is therefore no longer obligatory. While physician and patient have the permission (reshut) to utilize it, there is no moral requirement (mitzvah) that they do so.[40]

On this basis, halachists can permit the cessation of medical treatment for end-stage patients who have not arrived at brain death or to the point of gesisah, the very last moments of life. R. Moshe Feinstein rules that "when the physicians see that a person cannot recover from his illness but can only continue to live in a state of suffering; and when the treatment they prescribe serves only to prolong his life as it is now, filled with suffering; they must not administer the treatments but leave him alone." To support his decision, he cites the story of the last days of R. Yehudah Hanasi, or Rabbi, discussed above. Rabbi's maidservant, to use modern terminology, "pulled the plug" on prayers which had lost their therapeutic value.[41] Thus, we learn that there is a significant difference between healing (refu'ah) and medical procedures that needlessly prolong a patient's suffering; the former is obligatory, the latter is not.[42] R. Immanuel Jakobovits, too, rules that "there is no obligation to prolong the life and the suffering of a clearly terminal patient." He permits a diabetic who develops terminal, inoperable cancer to cease taking insulin. Although the insulin is a successful treatment for the diabetes, it can now only prolong his suffering and delay his death. This is true "even though he is not yet a *goses*; since the whole point of medicine is to restore a person's health, (the insulin) is no longer obligatory but merely voluntary."[43]

The standard of therapeutic effectiveness, as a tool by which to make judgments concerning medical treatment, allows us to draw some conclusions with moral confidence.

Under the heading "therapeutic" and "successful" treatments we would certainly include all medical and surgical procedures, such as antibiotics and routine surgeries, which physicians expect will lead to a cure for the illness in question. These treatments are "obligatory" under the traditional Jewish conception of medicine. Other therapies, though they do not produce a cure, would nonetheless fall under this category because they are able to control the disease and allow the patient a reasonable degree of function. Included here are such therapies as insulin for diabetes (so long as the patient has not developed another, terminal illness; see above) and dialysis for chronic renal disease. These procedures can be unpleasant, true, and they donot offer a cure, but they do offer life; they are to be considered as *pikuach nefesh*. When, however, a patient has entered the final stages of terminal disease, medical treatments and procedures which serve only to maintain this state of existence are not required. A cancer patient, for example, would accept radiation and/or chemotherapy so long as according to informed medical judgment these offer a reasonable prospect of curing, reversing, or controlling the cancer. Once this prospect has disappeared and the therapies can serve only to increase suffering by prolonging the patient's inevitable death from the disease, they are no longer to be regarded as medicine and may therefore be withdrawn.

While this standard is useful in helping to direct our thinking, it is by no means free of difficulty. Terms such as "therapeutic" and "successful treatment" are inherently vague and impossible to define with precision. In many situations it will be problematic if not impossible to determine when or even if the prescribed regime of therapy has lost its medical value. Yet the decision to continue or to cease the treatment must nonetheless be made, and those who must make it will confront an element of doubt and uncertainty that cannot be entirely resolved. Every such decision is inherently a matter of choice, a choice between two or more alternatives when none is the obviously correct one. This kind of uncertainty is disturbing to many, who believe (as do we all) that fundamental issues of life and death must be handled with an attitude of reverence and caution. Yet their laudable search for moral certainty has led some authorities toward an extremist position, rejecting the very possibility that treatment can ever be withdrawn from a dying patient. Says one: "every person is obligated in every case to seek out medical treatment, even though he believes that the treatment will not heal him but only prolong his suffering; for we must hope for and await God's deliverance to the very last moment of our lives."[44] This conviction is based upon the reasoning that, inasmuch as medicine is not a precise science, even the most definitive medical prognosis is a matter of *safek*, of doubt. We must work to preserve life until the very end, for while it can never be established with certainty that a patient has absolutely no hope for recovery, it is indeed certain that, should we withdraw medical care, the patient will die.[45]

To this argument we would simply ask: is this truly "medicine" as we conceive it? Our answer, as liberal Jews who seek guidance from our tradition in facing the moral dilemmas of our age, is "no." We do not adopt the simplistic approach, advocated by some, which holds that Jewish sacred texts have nothing to say to the challenges posed by contemporary medical reality. But we cannot and do not believe that those texts, which bid us to heal the sick and to preserve life, demand that in fulfilling these duties we apply in indiscriminate fashion every available technological device to prolong the death of a dying person. Medical science has made immeasurable advances during recent times, and we are thankful for that fact. Doctors today are able to prevent and to cure disease, to offer hope to the sick and disabled to an extent that past generations could scarcely imagine. Yet there comes a point in time when all the technologies, the chemicals, the surgeries, and the machines that comprise the lifesaving arsenal of modern medicine become counterproductive, a point when all that medical science can effectively do for a patient is to indefinitely delay his inevitable death. This is not *pikuach nefesh;* this is not medicine; this is not what physicians, as agents of healing, are supposed to do. There is neither meaning nor purpose in maintaining these treatments. They are salt on the tongue and the sound of a woodchopper. They are not *refu'ah;* no commandments are fulfilled thereby. Yes, life is a precious thing, and every moment of it should be regarded as God's gift. But we are not required under any reading of the tradition that makes sense to us to buy additional moments of life by undertaking useless and pointless medical treatment.

If this conviction leaves us in doubt as to the "right" answer for particular patients, then it is well to remember that moral, religious, and halachic truth can never be a matter of absolute certainty. There will always be more than one plausibly correct answer, more than one possible application of our texts and our values to the case at hand. Our task is to determine the best answer, the one that most closely corresponds to our understanding of the tradition as a whole. That search must be conducted by means of analysis, interpretation, and argument. Its outcome will never enjoy the finality of the solution to a mathematical equation; its conclusions will be subject to challenge and critique. Yet this is no reason to shrink from moral argument; it means rather that we have no choice but to enter the fray, to confront difficult cases, and to do the best we can. We may never be absolutely sure that we are "right"; but if we are thorough in our thinking, if we read the texts, consider the case, and conduct our argument carefully and prayerfully, then we can be sure that we have done our job.

IV. The Cases Before Us. We begin with Naomi. Canavan's Disease, a "spongy degeneration" of the central nervous system, usually occurs in infants of East European Jewish ancestry. It is characterized by progressive mental deterioration, spasticity, and blindness. Due to diminished chest muscle function, the child will often develop respiratory tract disease. Death will occur in most cases before the age of five. No means presently exist to cure or control the illness; "treatment is symptomatic and supportive."[46]

Based upon the analysis developed in the foregoing sections of this *t'shuvah,* we turn our attention to the nature and extent of this "symptomatic and supportive" treatment. Since Naomi's disease is a progressive one and can neither be reversed nor arrested, any measure that might be adduced to prolong her life is essentially an artificial and improper delay of her death and has no therapeutic value. For example, should she develop a respiratory tract disease, the goal of treatment need not be to "cure" that disease, since it is an integral part of a terminal illness which cannot be cured. She should receive treatments directed at relief of physical pain and suffering, so long as those treatments are not themselves so invasive as to increase her suffering. Naomi's parents are under no Jewish moral obligation to resort to any measures whose purpose it is to lengthen her life.

As for Esther, whose terminal illness has brought her to the very end of her life, it is clear that the family has no duty to administer "life-prolonging measures." By this we certainly mean "painful medical interventions," that offer no hope of arresting or controlling her Alzheimer's Disease. The issue of antibiotics is somewhat more difficult. On the one hand, these drugs do not affect the course of the Alzheimer's, which is causing her death; on the other hand, they would be considered "successful" treatments for the particular infections that afflict her. In this particular case, we would take the position advocated by Rabbi Jakobovits[47] and counsel that the antibiotics not be administered. We should remember that when we practice medicine, we are treating the *patient* and not this or that disease. The successful treatment of a particular infection in a terminal patient does not change the fact that the patient remains terminal and that death is inevitable. Antibiotics may be justified in cases where the patient's death is not imminent or when those drugs offer the prospect of restoring the patient to a reasonable degree of function. This latter judgment must, again, be measured not by the drug's effectiveness in controlling a specific, identifiable syndrome but rather in the context of the patient's total medical situation. Esther's advanced age and medical condition offer convincing evidence *both* that she is "terminal" and that death is relatively near. For such a patient, the antibiotics serve no reasonable therapeutic function; they are but pointless hindrances to her death.

V. On Artificial Nutrition and Hydration. The conclusion that medical treatment may be withdrawn or withheld raises a difficult question with respect to artificial nutrition and hydration. A terminal patient may be kept alive partially or even primarily by means of food and water supplied through tubes inserted into the veins, nose, or stomach. May we discontinue the supply of nutrients or disconnect the tubes altogether on the grounds that, as all hope for recovery or satisfactory control of the illness has vanished, this feeding serves only to prolong the patient's death?

The answer to this question depends upon whether we regard artificial nutrition and hydration as a "medical treatment." As we have seen, Jewish tradition offers strong support for the cessation of medical treatments for the terminally-ill when these treatments have lost their therapeutic effectiveness. We are not commanded to do medicine when our actions are *not* medicine, when they do not heal. We violate no moral obligation if we refuse to offer a patient drugs or technologies that are medically useless. By contrast, we do violate such an obligation under normal circumstances when we withhold food and water and thereby starve that person to death. Though we might respond that a patient fed through a tube hardly constitutes a "normal circumstance," artificial feeding differs from other hospital procedures in one crucial aspect: it can be argued that the feeding tube has nothing to do with "medicine" at all. Its function is not to treat the disease but to provide essential nutrients to the patient, and so long as the patient is capable of digesting these nutrients, the tube is successfully performing its task. In this analysis, artificial nutrition and hydration are not medical treatments, do not lose any "therapeutic" effectiveness, and therefore may not be withdrawn.

One could argue that artificial feeding devices are indeed "medical," a response to disease. They are utilized precisely because a patient is unable to ingest nutrients in the "normal" manner. As such they are medical interventions and can be withdrawn when the intervention is no longer medically justified. There is no reason to distinguish between feeding tubes and other, indisputable "medical" procedures such as cardiopulmonary resuscitation: both keep the terminal patient alive, and the withholding of either will result in death from the very disease that warranted its introduction in the first place. On the other hand, unlike sophisticated medical procedures, food and water are universal human needs. All of us, whether sick or well, require food and water in order to survive. Moreover, the fact that these nutrients are supplied by a machine does not transform them into exotic medical substances; we all receive our food at the end of a long chain of production, transportation, and distribution technologies. A real and desirable distinction can therefore be made between artificial feeding and medical treatment.

Opinions on this question are deeply divided. A broad coalition that includes medical ethicists, the American Medical Association,[48] and the United States Supreme Court[49] supports the definition of artificial nutrition and hydration as a medical procedure that may be withdrawn from terminal patients. On the other hand, this "emerging medical, ethical and legal consensus[50] has been challenged by some ethicists who argue that the withdrawal of nutrition resembles killing more than it does the cessation of purely "medical" treatment.[51] The dispute among halachic scholars is the mirror image of that among ethicists. Most authorities prohibit the withdrawal of food and water; "the reason, quite simply, is that eating is a normal physiological process, required to sustain life, necessary for all, including those who are healthy."[52] Food and water are not, therefore, medicine; their presence cannot be defined as medically illegitimate.[53] At the same time, some halachists have suggested the opposite, that artificial nutrition is a medical procedure and may be withdrawn.[54] Reform halachic opinion is also split: one responsum opposes the removal of the feeding tube,[55] though several others permit it.[56]

Given this division of opinion, we cannot claim that Jewish tradition categorically prohibits the withdrawal of food and water from dying patients. It can be plausibly argued that artificial nutrition and hydration are medical interventions which, on the Judaic grounds that we have cited in the previous two sections of this *t'shuvah*, may be discontinued upon a competent finding that they no longer provide therapeutic benefit to the patient. At the same time, we stress the plausibility of the opposing argument. Food and water, no matter how they are delivered, are the very staff of life *(lechem chuki)* for the human being. They sustain us at every moment of our lives, in health as well as in illness. It is therefore not at all obvious that we should look upon these substances as "medicine" merely because they come to us in the form of a tube inserted by medical professionals.[57] Moreover, the moral stakes in removing the feeding tube are considerable. As one authority who rules permissively admits, "there is something which is, minimally, highly unaesthetic" about withholding food and water from terminal patients.[58] We agree. Indeed, some of us would use stronger adjectives, for—let us neither mince words nor hide behind comforting euphemisms—we cannot overlook the fact that by removing them we are starving these human beings to death.[59]

We would therefore caution at the very least that the removal of artificial nutrition and hydration should never become a routine procedure. It is preferable that artificial feeding of terminal patients be maintained so that, when death comes, it will not have come because we have caused it by starvation. Nonetheless, because we cannot declare that cessation of artificial nutrition and hydration is categorically forbidden by Jewish moral thought, the patient and the family must ultimately let their conscience guide them in the choice between these two alternatives.

Excursus

As previously noted, supporters of euthanasia will cite various biblical and talmudic passages as evidence that the Jewish tradition supports a permissive stance toward mercy killing or, as it is called these days, physician-assisted suicide. We indicated in brief that the "tradition" does *not* so interpret those texts. That is to say, however Jews have read and understood the narratives of the deaths of King Saul, R. Chaninah ben Teradyon, and R. Yehudah Hanasi ("Rabbi"), these episodes have not tended to serve as "proof" that a terminally-ill patient may take active steps to end his or her life to avoid the sufferings of illness or that others may do so on behalf of the patient. We now want to examine this issue in some detail.

A. The Death of King Saul. While many commentators go to great lengths to justify Saul's suicide, they do so in a way which makes it difficult to use his case as a model for today's terminally-ill patient. Some write that Saul, as king of Israel, was a unique case, subject by the nature of his office to special ethical and political obligations that make it difficult to draw an analogy from his situation to any other. There was the concern, for example, that should Saul be captured alive the Israelites would have felt bound to attempt to rescue him, an attempt that would have entailed a severe loss of life and a further weakening of Israel's already-precarious military situation.[60] Others suggest that Saul took his life out of fear that his captors would torture him into committing the sin of idolatry; his death was thus an act of martyrdom and not simply an attempt to avoid suffering.[61] Still others reject the whole tradition which exonerates Saul: he committed suicide and bears the guilt of sin.[62]

B. The Death of R. Chaninah b. Teradyon. R. Chaninah b. Teradyon died a martyr's death at the hands of the Romans during the Hadrianic persecutions of the second century C.E.[63] According to the story, the Romans burned R. Chaninah at the stake, wrapped in the parchment of a *sefer Torah,* and they placed wet woolen rags around him in order to retard the flames and to prolong his agony. He nonetheless refuses to open his mouth and let the fire enter, in order to hasten his death; "it is better that the One who gives life take it away than for a person to bring harm upon himself." Yet when a Roman guard asks: "Rabbi, if I increase the flame and remove the rags, will you guarantee me life in the world to come?", R. Chaninah answers "yes," and the guard did so.

Since the guard's action hastens R. Chaninah's death, it is sometimes suggested that this narrative proves that we are permitted to do the same for the terminally ill. Yet if this is the case, if one may ask another to speed one's inevitable end, why does Chaninah himself not commit suicide? We cannot argue that an individual is forbidden to kill himself but may request others to do so, for such a conclusion runs counter to the most fundamental conceptions of moral responsibility. If I am forbidden to kill myself, I am not entitled to appoint another to kill me.[64] How then may R. Chaninah empower the guard to take this legal action? Traditional commentators resolve this contradiction by reminding us that the story of R. Chaninah is a case of martyrdom, for which, as we have seen, special rules apply.[65] The guard is not R. Chaninah's agent but his executioner; the rabbi cannot "appoint" the guard to do anything. The guard is the agent of the Roman authorities, who have the discretion to kill R. Chaninah according to their law or by any means they desire. The manner of R. Chaninah's death is not the "will of Heaven," "natural law," or any such thing; it is not up to him or subject to his decision. If the executioner decides to kill him more quickly, that is entirely the executioner's choice. What is up to R. Chaninah is the decision to participate directly in the hastening of his death, either by his own hand or through an agent; and this he does *not* do. This set of facts radically distinguishes the case of a martyr from that of the terminally-ill patient.

C. The Death of R. Yehudah Hanasi (Rabbi). When Rabbi is near death, his students gather to pray for his recovery.[66] His maidservant, who at first is sympathetic to their efforts, soon realizes that Rabbi is beyond the point of healing; the time of his death is nigh, and the prayers serve only to his suffering. She therefore prays that Rabbi die quickly. When she sees that the students will not cease their own prayers, she casts a glass vessel from the attic of the house to the ground; the startling sound interrupts the prayers, and Rabbi dies.

Again, some read the story as an example of mercy killing; therefore, they argue that this story provides support for the practice of euthanasia for those like Rabbi suffering the end-stage of terminal disease. The rabbinic tradition, as we have seen,[67] adopts a different interpretation: the maidservant did not kill Rabbi but rather removed an inappropriate impediment to his death. Advocates of mercy killing reject this distinction as excessively formalistic. They claim there is no significant moral difference between taking action to hasten a person's death and withdrawing treatment so as to allow death to occur; both of these are positive actions which speed the death of the patient. We would reject this claim on two grounds. First, Jewish ethical thought does see a significant difference between action that directly kills a person and inaction which allows him to die.[68] And second, as we have argued above, the removal of an impediment is not an act of killing at all, even passive killing, but in fact a corrective measure taken against a situation that we have wrongly allowed to occur. For while Jewish tradition forbids us to kill a terminal patient it also forbids us to delay her death unnecessarily. It is therefore permitted to remove factors which contribute to that delay. To permit mercy killing, however, would be to permit the taking of a life even in the absence of "impediments" (machines, medications, etc.) that serve no therapeutic effect other than to delay death. Such killing is qualitatively distinct from the removal of an impediment.

NOTES

1 See the essays by Rabbi Leonard Kravitz and Peter Knobel in Walter Jacob and Moshe Zemer, eds., *Death and Euthanasia in Jewish Law* (Pittsburgh and Tel Aviv, 1995).

2 This is evident from the Hebrew term for "suicide": *hame'abed atsmo leda'at*; see *Sh. A.* YD 345:2–3 and commentaries *ad loc.*

3 See *Yad,* Hilchot Rotzeach 1:4.

4 See the commentary of R. David ibn Zimra to *Yad,* Sanhedrin 18:6, printed editions. For the prohibition of suicide, see BT Baba Kama 91b (the midrash on Gen. 9:5, and see Rashi, *ad loc.*) and *Yad,* Hilchot Rozseach 2:2–3. For that matter, one is not entitled to subject his/her body to physical damage *(chabalah),* a principle so well established that the permissibility of cosmetic surgery is a matter of no little controversy within the legal literature. BT Baba Kama 90b; *Yad,* Hilchot Chovel 5:1; *Sh. A.,* CM 420:31.

5 See Rambam, Commentary to M. 'Arachin 1:3.

6 *Sh. A.,* YD 329:4. This ruling seems odd at first glance because the permit to violate the laws of Shabbat is based upon Leviticus 18:5: "these are the laws...which a person shall perform and *live by them...*" (BT Yoma 85b). Surely the *goses,* who stands at the brink of death, cannot "live" by these laws for more than a few hours or, at the very most, days. Yet see *Mishnah Berurah, Be'ur Halachah, s.v. 'ela lefi sh.a. 'ah:* we violate Shabbat for the *goses* because the Torah places inestimable value upon even the briefest span of human life.

7 BT Sanhedrin 78a; *Yad,* Hilchot Rotzeach 2:7

8 M. Semachot 1:4; *Yad,* Hilchot Avel 4:5; *Alfasi,* BT Mo'ed Katan, fol. 16b; *Sh. A.* YD 339:1.

9 Some authorities point to the *tereifah,* the person who is terminally ill and should die within one year, as a major exception to this rule: according to Jewish law, the one who kills a *tereifah* is not punished by death as is the killer of the *goses.* However we try to resolve this apparent contradiction, we should not forget that while the killer of the *tereifah* is exempt from execution by the earthly court, he has still committed a serious moral offense that will presumably bring heavenly retribution in its wake. It is arguably possible to rank the *tereifah* lower than the healthy person on a scale of priorities in *pikuach nefesh;* i.e., I may be entitled to save the healthy person before I aid the *tereifah.* Still, it is *not permitted* to kill the *tereifah,* a point of no little significance in the debate over euthanasia. See BT Sanh. 78a and *Yad,* Hilchot Rotzeach 2:7–9.

10 BT Sanhedrin 74a–b and parallels; *Yad,* Hilchot Yesodey HaTorah 5:1–4; YD 157:1. The sources add that during a time of religious persecution a Jew must accept martyrdom rather than transgress even the smallest detail of customary Jewish observance. Some authorities permit an individual to accept martyrdom even in situations where the law does not require one to do so; see *Hil. HaRosh,* Avodah Zarah 2:9.

11 Rabbeinu Tam in Tosafot, Avodah Zarah 18a, s.v. *ve'al,* citing the story of the captive children in BT Gittin 57b (and see Tosafot Gittin 57b, *s.v. kaftsu*). By the early fourteenth century, such acts of suicide had been approved by leading rabbinic authorities; see *Hiddushey HaRitva,* Avodah Zarah 18a. See, in general, R. Yosef Karo's Bedek HaBayit to *Tur* YD 157.

12 R. David Kimchi *ad loc.,* citing Bereshit Rabah 34:13, which exempts cases "like that of King Saul" from the prohibition against suicide derived from Genesis 9:5 (see note 4, above).

13 *Sh. A.,* YD 345:3. See also *R. Shalom Schwadron, Resp. Maharsham,* v. 6, YD, no. 123, who explicitly rejects the opposing view of the Hatam Sofer (*Responsa,* YD, no. 326). A similar position is taken by two of Sofer's early 19th-century contemporaries: R. Efraim Margoliot, *Resp. Beit Efraim,* YD, no. 76, and R. Mordechai Benet, *Resp. Parashat Mordechai,* YD, no. 25-26.

14 *Aruch HaShulchan,* YD 345, no. 5: Saul's suicide was a case of emotional coercion *(ones)* and not a rational choice. See in general *SA, YD* 345:3 and *Pitchey Teshuvah,* no. 3.

15 Those who advocate euthanasia sometimes attempt to distinguish between an "agadic tradition" which tells stories that support mercy killing and a "halachic tradition" which opposes it. We think this attempt is fruitless. Both literary genres are the product of the same religious culture; the rabbis who tell the stories are the same rabbis who read them to learn the law. And it is those rabbis who prohibit euthanasia.

16 Our own Reform responsa tradition, it should be noted, has consistently rejected euthanasia as a morally acceptable response to terminal illness. See the *t'shuvot* of R. Israel Bettan (*ARR,* no. 78, pp. 261-271), R. Solomon B. Freehof (*ARR,* no. 77, pp. 257-260; *Reform Responsa,* no. 27, pp. 117-122; *Modern Reform Responsa,* no. 34, pp. 188-197, 35, pp. 197-203), R. Walter Jacob (*ARR,* no. 79, pp. 271-274; *CARR,* no. 81, pp. 135-136, 83, pp. 138-140; *Questions and Reform Jewish Answers,* no. 145, pp., 157, pp. 259-262), R. Moshe Zemer (*Halachah Shefuyah,* pp. 295-298).

17 Hence, the blessing *dayan ha'emet,* "blessed be...the True Judge," traditionally recited at the death of a relative or when one receives evil tidings. See M. Berachot 9:5: the commandment to love God "with all your strength" (Deut. 6:5) implies that we are to give expression to this love come what may. See also *Yad,* Hilchot Berachot 10:3, and *Sh. A.,* OC 222:2. This does not mean that we must accept sorrow and tragedy in passivity; the numerous stories of Jewish heroes who "argue with God" against the evil in the world are sufficient proof of that. It does suggest, however, that the experience of evil does not bring an end to the very relationship with God in which a meaningful argument can take place.

18 Report of the Board of Trustees of the American Medical Association in *Issues in Law and Medicine* 10:1 (Summer, 1994), pp. 89ff, at p. 91. See also at p. 81: "The Board of Trustees recommends that the American Medical Association reject euthanasia and physician-assisted suicide as being incompatible with the nature and purposes of the healing arts." While Dutch observers report that there is some controversy over these statistics, that controversy in no way lessens the moral gravity of the situation. On the case of the Netherlands, see the article by Joop Al in *Jewish Law Annual,* v. 12.

19 R. Ya'akov Emden (18th century), *Mor uKetzi'ah,* ch. 328.

20 R. Eliezer Waldenberg, *Resp. Tzitz Eliezer*, v. 13, no. 87. Waldenberg cautions that the intent of the procedure must be to relieve pain and not to hasten the patient's death, a point made as well by Emden, note 19, above.

21 Ch. 723 (= ch. 315, Wistinetzki-Freimann, ed.)

22 *Turey Zahav*, YD *ad loc.* He notes that Karo's ruling, to which Isserles does not object, prohibits even the closing of the patient's eyelids at the moment of death. The slightest amount of contact, therefore, must be seen as the hastening of death.

23 *Nekudot HaKesef ad loc.*

24 *Shiltey Giborim* to Rif, Mo'ed Katan, fol. 16. It should be noted that R. Yehoshua Boaz, an older contemporary of Isserles, never saw the latter's ruling. He is addressing the same contradiction as it appears in *Sefer Chasidim.* The thrust of his comment is applied to Isserles by *Beit Lechem Yehudah*, YD 339.

25 *Sefer Chasidim loc. cit.*

26 For this reason, too, the *Shiltey Giborim* supports the prohibition against moving the mattress. Even though the feathers may serve to impede the patient's death, the mattress itself is supposed to be there; it pays a legitimate role in the care of the *goses*, and is thus not solely an impediment that must be removed.

27 See R. Eliezer Yehudah Waldenberg, *Resp. Tzitz Eliezer*, vol. 13, no. 89. Waldenberg conditions this permit upon the performance of extensive test which show that the patient cannot recover independent respiration. See also R. Chaim David Halevy, *Aseh Lecha Rav*, v. 5, no. 29.

28 Rabbi B. Rabinovits, *Sefer Asya*, 1976, pp. 197-198.

29 Dr. Ya'akov Levy, *No'am*, vol. 16, 1973, pp. 53ff.

30 Thus, Waldenberg (see above, n. 24) stresses that his permission to turn off the respirator applies only at the very end of life *(gemer kalot hanefesh.)*

31 BT Baba Kama 85a. "Permission" is necessary, according to Nachmanides (see n. 29, below), for two reasons: in order to protect the physician from claims of liability should be cause injury to the patient, and in order to allow the practice of healing even when it seems to contradict the Divine will ("if God smites a person, who am I to heal him?").

32 Ramban, *Torat Ha'Adam*, Chavel ed., pp. 41-42. His discussion forms the basis of the Tur, YD 336, on the laws of medicine. On *pikuach nefesh* see Lev. 18:5 and BT Yoma 85b.

33 Rambam, *Commentary to the Mishnah*, Nedarim 4:4. The verse declares that we are obligated to restore a lost object to its rightful owner; the midrash cites a linguistic peculiarity in the verse to extend this duty to the "restoration/rescue of a person's life" (hashevat gufo; BT Sanhedrin 73a). See the discussion in our responsum 5754.18. "Physicians and Indigent Patients," below.

34 *Yad*, Rotzeach 1:14. On "not standing idly by..." see Lev. 19:16 and BT Sanhedrin 73a.

35 Maimonides, *Commentary to the Mishnah ad loc.*

36 M. Baba Kama 8:5; BT Baba Kama 91a–b; *Yad*, Hilchot Chovel 5:1; *Sh. A., CM* 420:31. See, in general, our responsum 5752.7, "On the Permissibility of Cosmetic Surgery," above.

37 See at note 19, above.

38 *Resp. R. David ibn Zimra* (16th-c. Egypt), v. 1, no. 1139.

39 R. Ya'kov Emden, *Mor uKetzi'ah*, 328; R. Moshe Raziel, *"Kefi'at choleh lekabel tipul refu'i,"* Techumin 2 (1981), 335-336.

40 See R. Ya'akov b. Shmuel (Prussia, 17th century), *Resp. Beit Ya'akov*, no. 59. R. Ya'akov Reischer (Germany, 18th century) in his *Resp. Shevut Ya'akov*, OC no. 13, disputes the *Beit Ya'akov*, but only in that he regards it permissible *(mutar)* for a physician to administer medications that delay death. He does not claim that it is obligatory to do so.

41 R. Nissim Gerondi, *Commentary to BT Nedarim* 40a, also cited this story as an halachic precedent, but in a more restrictive sense: since the maidservant, seeing Rabbi in excruciating pain, had previously prayed for his speedy death, R. Nissim learns that there are times when one is permitted to pray for the death of a suffering patient. Feinstein goes farther, suggesting that the story serves as a precedent for the cessation of medical treatment.

42 *Resp. Igrot Moshe*, CM, v. 2, no. 73–74.

43 Rabbi I. Jakobovits, in *HaPardes* 31 (1957), no. 3, pp. 18–19

44 R. Natan Zvi Friedman, *Resp. Netser Mata'i*, no. 30. See also R. Eliezer Yehudah Waldenberg, *Resp. Tzitz Eliezer*, vol. 5, Ramat Rachel, no. 28, and J.D. Bleich, "The Quinlan Case: A Jewish Perspective," in Fred Rosner and J. David Bleich, eds., *Jewish Bioethics* (New York, 1979), pp. 266–276.

45 See R. Avraham Yitschak Hakohen Kook, *Resp. Da'at Kohen*, no. 142; *Resp. Chatam Sofer*, YD, no. 158.

46 J.G. Theone, *Physicians' Guide to Rare Diseases* (Montvale, NJ: 1992), pp. 373–373. See also J.B. Wyngaarden and C.H. Smith, Jr., eds., *The Cecil Textbook of Medicine*, 18th edition (Philadelphia, 1988), p. 2216.

47 At note 43, above.

48 Council on Ethical and Judicial Affairs of the American Medical Association, *Opinions* (Chicago: 1986), Opinion 2:20.

49 *Cruzan v. Director, Missouri Department of Health*, 497 U.S. 261 (1990)

50 The term is that of Robert Steinbrook and Bernard Lo, "Artificial Feeding—Solid Ground, Not a Slippery Slope," *New England Journal of Medicine* 319 (1988), p. 288.

51 See Patrick G. Derr, "Why Food and Fluids Can Never Be Denied," *Hastings Center Report* 16 (February, 1986), pp. 28–30; Gilbert Mailaender, "On Removing Food and Water: Against the Stream," *Hastings Center Report* 14 (December, 1984), pp. 11–13; Daniel Callahan, "On Feeding the Dying," *Hastings Center Report* 13 (October, 1983), p. 22.

52 R. Moshe Feinstein, *Resp. Igrot Moshe*, CM, v. 2, no. 74, sec. 3.

53 See *Nishmat Avraham, YD 339*, pp. 245-346; Avraham Steinberg in *Sefer Asya* 3 (1983), p. 448; R. Immanuel Jakobovits in *HaPardes* 31:3 (1957), pp. 18–19. Among Conservative thinkers see R. David Feldman, *Health and Medicine in the Jewish Tradition* (New York, 1986), p. 95, and R. Avram Reisner in *Conservative Judaism* 43:3 (1991), pp. 52ff.

54 For Orthodox opinion, see R. Zev Schostak, "Jewish Ethical Guidelines for Resuscitation and Artificial Nutrition and Hydration of the Dying Elderly," *Journal of Medical Ethics* 20:2 (June, 1994), p. 98, and R. Zalman Goldberg in *Emek Halachah (Asya)* (Jerusalem, 1986), p. 78 (but see note 13 ad loc.). An important Conservative responsum in this vein is authored by R. Elliot N. Dorff in *Conservative Judaism* 43:3 (1991), pp. 36–39.

55 See "Hospital Patient Beyond Recovery," below.

56 R. Walter Jacob, *Questions and Reform Jewish Answers*, no. 159, pp. 263–269; R. Mark N. Staitman in Jacob and Zemer, *Death and Euthanasia*, pp. 1–10. See also R. Solomon Freehof, in *ARR*, no. 77, pp. 257–260, who permits the physician to refrain from connecting or refilling the nutrition apparatus of a dying patient.

57 The argument, advanced by some, that we are not obligated to provide artificial nutrition because it is essentially different from "eating" in the normal sense is hard to understand. In either case, whether we prevent a healthy person from eating or withdraw artificial nutrition from a patient, we are withholding nutrients that are necessary for survival and starving that person to death.

58 *Dorff*, note 56, above, at 38.

59 The *Cruzan* case (see n. 51, above) is instructive here. Though Ms. Cruzan's parents sought to discontinue artificial feeding, they did not ask for the removal of the feeding tube, which they wanted left in place so that medications might be administered to reduce seizures as their daughter died. That is to say, they did not ask to discontinue her medical treatment so that "nature" might take its course; they asked that food and water be withheld so as to cause her death by starvation.

60 See R. Shelomo Luria, *Yam shel Shelomo*, Baba Kama, ch. 8, no. 59.

61 *Hiddushey HaRitva*, Avodah Zarah 18a. See above at notes 10 and 11.

62 See R. Yosef Karo, Bedek haBayit, *Tur* YD 157.

63 BT Avodah Zarah 18a.

64 The operative principle is *shelucho shel adam kemoto*, "one's agent is the legal equivalent of oneself." A person's legal representative, who carries that person's "power of attorney," is endowed with only those rights enjoyed by the one who appointed him or her. A corollary is the statement *ein shaliach ledevar aveirah*: "an agent cannot legally perform a transgression." Should I instruct my agent to do something prohibited by the Torah, those instructions are null and void; BT Kiddushin 41b–42b and parallels.

65 See above at notes 10 and 11.

66 BT Ketubot 104a.

67 See above, at notes 41–42.

68 The classic example is the case in BT Sanhedrin 74a, where one has been told: kill so-and-so; if you refuse, we will kill you. The ruling in that instance: let yourself be killed. How do you know that your blood is redder than his? Perhaps his blood is redder. That is, the lives of both are equally precious to God. One life will be destroyed in either event; do not compound the tragedy by committing the sin of murder (see Rashi *ad loc.*). The only proper moral stance is *shev ve'al ta'aseh,* inaction, for positive action can but make the situation worse.

9

Resources and Bibliography

Health Care Powers of Attorney

American Association of Retired Persons
1909 K Street, N.W., Washington, DC 20049

or

American Bar Association
Commission on Legal Problems of the Elderly
1800 M. Street, N.W., Washington, DC 20036

National Institute for Jewish Hospice
Cedars-Sinai Medical Center
Suite 652, 8723 Alden Drive, Los Angeles, CA 90048

Sample Advance Directive

Rabbinic Council of America
275 Seventh Ave., New York, NY 10001

Tomorrow's Choices: Preparing Now for Future Legal, Financial, and Health Care Decisions

American Association of Retired Persons
1909 K Street, N.W., Washington, DC 20049

UAHC Committee on Bio-ethics: Department of Jewish Family Concerns
Rabbi Richard F. Address
633 Third Ave., New York, NY 10017

Bibliography

Abrahams, Israel, ed. *Hebrew Ethical Wills*. Philadelphia: Jewish Publication Society, 1926.

Address, Richard. "Making Sacred Choices at the End of Life." *Life Lights*. Woodstock, VT: Jewish Lights Publishing, 2000.

Brenner, Anne. *Mourning and Mitzvah*. Woodstock, VT: Jewish Lights Publishing, 1993.

Callahan, Daniel. *The Troubled Dream of Life: Living with Mortality*. New York: Simon & Schuster, 1993.

Dorff, Elliot N. *Matters of Life and Death: A Jewish Approach To Modern Medical Ethics*. Philadelphia: Jewish Publication Society, 1998.

Dworkin, Ronald. *Life's Dominion: An Argument About Abortion, Euthanasia, and Individual Freedom*. New York: Alfred A. Knopf, 1993.

Emanuel, Linda L. and Ezekiel J. Emanuel. "The Medical Directive," *Journal of the American Medical Association* Vol. 261, No. 22 (June 9, 1989).

Gordon, Harvey. *When It Hurts Too Much To Live: Questions and Answers About Jewish Tradition and the Issues of Assisted Death*. New York: Union of American Hebrew Congregations Department of Jewish Family Concerns, 1998.

Grollman, Earl A. *Concerning Death: A Practical Guide for the Living*. Boston: Beacon Press, 1974
_____. *Talking About Death: A Dialogue Between Parent and Child*. Boston: Beacon Press, 1974.

Heschel, Abraham Joshua. *Between Man and God*. New York: The Free Press, 1959.

Jacob, Walter, ed. *American Reform Responsa*. New York: CCAR Press, 1983.

_____. *Contemporary American Reform Responsa*. New York: CCAR Press, 1997

Jacob, Walter and Moshe Zemer, eds. *Death and Euthanasia in Jewish Law*. Pittsburgh: Freehof Institute for Progressive Halakha/Rodef Shalom Press, 1994.

Kogan, Barry. *A Time To Be Born and a Time To Die.* Hawthorne, NY: Walter De Gruyter, 1991.

Liebman, Joshua Loth. *Peace of Mind.* New York: Simon & Schuster, 1946.

Maslin, Simeon J., ed. *Gates of Mitzvah.* New York: CCAR Press, 1979.

Nuland, Sherwin B. *How We Die: Reflections on Life's Final Chapter.* New York: Alfred A. Knopf, 1993.

Plaut, W. Gunther and Mark Washofsky. *Teshuvot for the Nineties.* New York: CCAR Press, 1997.

Reimer, Jack and Nathaniel Stampfler, eds. *So That Your Values Live On: Ethical Wills and How to Prepare Them.* Woodstock, VT: Jewish Lights Publishing, 1991.

Rosner, Fred. *Modern Medicine and Jewish Ethics. 2nd ed.* Hoboken, NJ: K'tav, and New York: Yeshiva University Press, 1991.

Sinclair, Daniel. *Tradition and the Biological Revolution.* Edinburgh, Scotland: Edinburgh University Press, 1989.

Stern, Chaim, ed. *Gates of Repentance.* New York: CCAR Press, 1978.
_____. *The Gates of the House.* New York: CCAR Press, 1976.

Syme, Daniel B. *The Jewish Home.* New York: UAHC Press, 1988.

Tendler, Moshe and Fred Rosner. "Quality and Sanctity of Life in the Talmud and Midrash." *Tradition* 1 (28), 1993.

UAHC Committee on Bio-ethics Program/Case Study II
"Autonomy: My Right to Live or Die," April 1990

UAHC Committee on Bio-ethics Program/Case Study III
"Termination of Treatment," April 1990

UAHC Committee on Bio-ethics Program/Case Study IV
"The Living Will," January 1991

UAHC Committee on Bio-ethics Program/Case Study V
"Assisted Suicide/Voluntary Active Euthanasia," Summer 1993

Union of American Hebrew Congregations. "The Living Will: Advance Medical Directives." New York: UAHC Bio-ethics Study Guide IV, 1991.

_____ "The Role of Pain and Suffering in Decision Making." New York: UAHC Bio-ethics Study Guide VIII, 1996.

_____. "To Everything There is a Season: Congregational Funeral and Cemetery Policies and Practices." Department of Synagogue Management, 2001.

10

The Advance Directive/Health Care Proxy Forms

The Medical Directive

Introduction. As part of a person's right to self-determination, every adult may accept or refuse any recommended medical treatment. This is relatively easy when people are well and can speak. Unfortunately, during serious illness they are often unconscious or otherwise unable to communicate their wishes—at the very time when many critical decisions need to be made.

The Medical Directive allows you to record your wishes regarding various types of medical treatments in several representative situations so that your desires can be respected. It also lets you appoint a proxy, someone to make medical decisions in your place if you should become unable to make them on your own.

The Medical Directive comes into effect only if you become incompetent (unable to make decisions and too sick to have wishes). You can change it at any time until then. As long as you are competent, you should discuss your care directly with your physician.

Completing the form. You should, if possible complete the form in the context of a discussion with your physician. Ideally, this should occur in the presence of your proxy. This lets your physician and your proxy know how you think about these decisions, and it provides you and your physician with the opportunity to give or clarify relevant personal or medical information. You may also wish to discuss the issues with your family, friends, or religious mentor.

The Medical Directive contains six illness situations that include incompetence. For each one, you consider possible interventions and goals of medical care. Situation A is permanent coma; B is near death; C is with weeks to live in and out of consciousness; D is extreme dementia; E is a situation you describe; and F is temporary inability to make decisions.

For each scenario you identify your general goals for care and specific intervention choices. The interventions are divided into six groups: 1) cardiopulmonary resuscitation or major surgery; 2) mechanical breathing or dialysis; 3) blood transfusions or blood products; 4) artificial nutrition and hydration; 5) simple diagnostic tests or antibiotics; and 6) pain medications, even if they dull consciousness and indirectly shorten life. Most of these treatments are described briefly. If you have further questions, consult your physician.

Your wishes for treatment options (I want this treatment; I want this treatment tried, but stopped if there is no clear improvement; I am undecided; I do not want this treatment) should be indicated. If you choose a trial of treatment, you should understand that this indicates you want the treatment *withdrawn* if your physician and proxy believe that it has become futile.

The Personal Statement section allows you to explain your choices, and say anything you wish to those who may make decisions for you concerning the limits of your life and the goals of intervention. For example, in situation B, if you wish to define "uncertain chance" with numerical probability, you may do so here.

Next you may express your preferences concerning organ donation. Do you wish to donate your body or some or all of your organs after your death? If so, for what purpose(s) and to which physician or institution? If not, this should also be indicated in the appropriate box.

In the final section you may designate one or more proxies, who would be asked to make choices under circumstances in which your wishes are unclear. You can indicate whether or not the decisions of the proxy should override your wishes if there are differences. And, should you name more than one proxy, you can state who is to have the final say if there is disagreement. Your proxy must understand that this role usually involves making judgments that you would have made for yourself, had you been able—and making them by the criteria you have outlined. Proxy decisions should ideally be made in discussion with your family, friends, and physician.

What to do with the form. Once you have completed the form, you and two adult witnesses (other than your proxy) who have no interest in your estate need to sign and date it.

Many states have legislation covering documents of this sort. To determine the laws in your state, you should call the state attorney general's office or consult a lawyer. If your state has a statutory document, you may wish to use the Medical Directive and append it to this form.

You should give a copy of the completed document to your physician. His or her signature is desirable but not mandatory. The Directive should be placed in your medical records and flagged so that anyone who might be involved in your care can be aware of its presence. Your proxy, a family member, and/or a friend should also have a copy. In addition, you may want to carry a wallet card noting that you have such a document and where it can be found.

An earlier version of this form was originally published as part of an article by Linda L. Emanuel and Ezekiel J. Emanuel, "The Medical Directive: A New Comprehensive Advance Care Document," *Journal of the American Medical Association* 261:3288–3293, June 9, 1989. It does not reflect the official policy of the American Medical Association.

My Medical Directive

This Medical Directive shall stand as a guide to my wishes regarding medical treatments in the event that illness should make me unable to communicate them directly. I make this Directive, being 18 years or more of age, of sound mind, and appreciating the consequences of my decisions.

SITUATION A

If I am in a coma or a persistent vegetative state and, in the opinion of my physician and two consultants, have no known hope of regaining awareness and higher mental functions no matter what is done, then my goals and specific wishes—if medically reasonable—for this and any additional illness would be:

☐   prolong life; treat everything
☐   attempt to cure, but reevaluate often
☐   limit to less invasive and less burdensome interventions
☐   provide comfort care only
☐   other (please specify):_____

Please check appropriate boxes:	I want	I want treatment tried. If no clear improvement, stop.	I am undecided	I do not want
1. **Cardiopulmonary resuscitation** (chest compressions, drugs, electric shocks, and artificial breathing aimed at reviving a person who is on the point of dying).		*Not applicable*		
2. **Major surgery** (for example, removing the gallbladder or part of the colon).		*Not applicable*		
3. **Mechanical breathing** (respiration by machine, through a tube in the throat).				
4. **Dialysis** (cleaning the blood by machine or by fluid passed through the belly).				
5. **Blood transfusions or blood products.**		*Not applicable*		
6. **Artificial nutrition and hydration** (given through a tube in a vein or in the stomach).				
7. **Simple diagnostic tests** (for example, blood tests or x-rays).		*Not applicable*		
8. **Antibiotics** (drugs used to fight infection).		*Not applicable*		
9. **Pain medications, even if they dull consciousness and indirectly shorten my life.**		*Not applicable*		

SITUATION B

If I am near death and in a coma and, in the opinion of my physician and two consultants, have a small but uncertain chance of regaining higher mental functions, a somewhat greater chance of surviving with permanent mental and physical disability, and a much greater chance of not recovering at all, then my goals and specific wishes—if medically reasonable—for this and any additional illness would be:

☐   prolong life; treat everything
☐   attempt to cure, but reevaluate often
☐   limit to less invasive and less burdensome interventions
☐   provide comfort care only
☐   other *(please specify):*_____

Please check appropriate boxes:	I want	I want treatment tried. If no clear improvement, stop.	I am undecided	I do not want
1. **Cardiopulmonary resuscitation** (chest compressions, drugs, electric shocks, and artificial breathing aimed at reviving a person who is on the point of dying).		*Not applicable*		
2. **Major surgery** (for example, removing the gallbladder or part of the colon).		*Not applicable*		
3. **Mechanical breathing** (respiration by machine, through a tube in the throat).				
4. **Dialysis** (cleaning the blood by machine or by fluid passed through the belly).				
5. **Blood transfusions or blood products.**		*Not applicable*		
6. **Artificial nutrition and hydration** (given through a tube in a vein or in the stomach).				
7. **Simple diagnostic tests** (for example, blood tests or x-rays).		*Not applicable*		
8. **Antibiotics** (drugs used to fight infection).		*Not applicable*		
9. **Pain medications, even if they dull consciousness and indirectly shorten my life.**		*Not applicable*		

Situation C

If I have a terminal illness with weeks to live, and my mind is not working well enough to make decisions for myself, but I am sometimes awake and seem to have feelings, then my goals and specific wishes—if medically reasonable—for this and any additional illness would be:

*In this state, prior wishes need to be balanced with a best guess about your current feelings. The proxy and physician have to make this judgment for you.

☐   prolong life; treat everything
☐   attempt to cure, but reevaluate often
☐   limit to less invasive and less burdensome interventions
☐   provide comfort care only
☐   other *(please specify):*_____

Please check appropriate boxes:	I want	I want treatment tried. If no clear improvement, stop.	I am undecided	I do not want
1. **Cardiopulmonary resuscitation** (chest compressions, drugs, electric shocks, and artificial breathing aimed at reviving a person who is on the point of dying).		*Not applicable*		
2. **Major surgery** (for example, removing the gallbladder or part of the colon).		*Not applicable*		
3. **Mechanical breathing** (respiration by machine, through a tube in the throat).				
4. **Dialysis** (cleaning the blood by machine or by fluid passed through the belly).				
5. **Blood transfusions or blood products.**		*Not applicable*		
6. **Artificial nutrition and hydration** (given through a tube in a vein or in the stomach).				
7. **Simple diagnostic tests** (for example, blood tests or x-rays).		*Not applicable*		
8. **Antibiotics** (drugs used to fight infection).		*Not applicable*		
9. **Pain medications, even if they dull consciousness and indirectly shorten my life.**		*Not applicable*		

SITUATION D

If I have brain damage or some brain disease that in the opinion of my physician and two consultants cannot be reversed and that makes me unable to think or have feelings, *but I have no terminal illness*, then my goals and specific wishes—if medically reasonable—for this and any additional illness would be:

☐   prolong life; treat everything
☐   attempt to cure, but reevaluate often
☐   limit to less invasive and less burdensome interventions
☐   provide comfort care only
☐   other *(please specify):*_____

Please check appropriate boxes:	I want	I want treatment tried. If no clear improvement, stop.	I am undecided	I do not want
1. **Cardiopulmonary resuscitation** (chest compressions, drugs, electric shocks, and artificial breathing aimed at reviving a person who is on the point of dying).		*Not applicable*		
2. **Major surgery** (for example, removing the gallbladder or part of the colon).		*Not applicable*		
3. **Mechanical breathing** (respiration by machine, through a tube in the throat).				
4. **Dialysis** (cleaning the blood by machine or by fluid passed through the belly).				
5. **Blood transfusions or blood products.**		*Not applicable*		
6. **Artificial nutrition and hydration** (given through a tube in a vein or in the stomach).				
7. **Simple diagnostic tests** (for example, blood tests or x-rays).		*Not applicable*		
8. **Antibiotics** (drugs used to fight infection).		*Not applicable*		
9. **Pain medications, even if they dull consciousness and indirectly shorten my life.**		*Not applicable*		

SITUATION E

If I . . .

(describe a situation that is important to you and/or your doctor believes you should consider in view of your current medical situation):

☐   prolong life; treat everything

☐   attempt to cure, but reevaluate often

☐   limit to less invasive and less burdensome interventions

☐   provide comfort care only

☐   other *(please specify):*_____

Please check appropriate boxes:	I want	I want treatment tried. If no clear improvement, stop.	I am undecided	I do not want
1. **Cardiopulmonary resuscitation** (chest compressions, drugs, electric shocks, and artificial breathing aimed at reviving a person who is on the point of dying).		*Not applicable*		
2. **Major surgery** (for example, removing the gallbladder or part of the colon).		*Not applicable*		
3. **Mechanical breathing** (respiration by machine, through a tube in the throat).				
4. **Dialysis** (cleaning the blood by machine or by fluid passed through the belly).				
5. **Blood transfusions or blood products.**		*Not applicable*		
6. **Artificial nutrition and hydration** (given through a tube in a vein or in the stomach).				
7. **Simple diagnostic tests** (for example, blood tests or x-rays).		*Not applicable*		
8. **Antibiotics** (drugs used to fight infection).		*Not applicable*		
9. **Pain medications, even if they dull consciousness and indirectly shorten my life.**		*Not applicable*		

SITUATION F

If I am in my current state of health (describe briefly): _____

_____

_____

and then have an illness that, in the opinion of my physician and two consultants, is life threatening but reversible, and I am temporarily unable to make decisions, then my goals and specific wishes—if medically reasonable—would be:

☐ prolong life; treat everything
☐ attempt to cure, but reevaluate often
☐ limit to less invasive and less burdensome interventions
☐ provide comfort care only
☐ other *(please specify)*:_____

Please check appropriate boxes:	I want	I want treatment tried. If no clear improvement, stop.	I am undecided	I do not want
1. **Cardiopulmonary resuscitation** (chest compressions, drugs, electric shocks, and artificial breathing aimed at reviving a person who is on the point of dying).		*Not applicable*		
2. **Major surgery** (for example, removing the gallbladder or part of the colon).		*Not applicable*		
3. **Mechanical breathing** (respiration by machine, through a tube in the throat).				
4. **Dialysis** (cleaning the blood by machine or by fluid passed through the belly).				
5. **Blood transfusions or blood products.**		*Not applicable*		
6. **Artificial nutrition and hydration** (given through a tube in a vein or in the stomach).				
7. **Simple diagnostic tests** (for example, blood tests or x-rays).		*Not applicable*		
8. **Antibiotics** (drugs used to fight infection).		*Not applicable*		
9. **Pain medications, even if they dull consciousness and indirectly shorten my life.**		*Not applicable*		

My Personal Statement

Please mention anything that would be important for your physician and your proxy to know. In particular, try to answer the following questions: 1) What medical conditions, if any, would make living so unpleasant that you would want life-sustaining treatment *withheld?* (Intractable pain? Irreversible mental damage? Inability to share love? Dependence on others? Another condition you would regard as intolerable?) 2) Under what medical circumstances would you want to stop interventions that might already have been started? 3) Why do you choose what you choose?

If there is any difference between my preferences detailed in the illness situations and those understood from my goals or from my personal statement, I wish my treatment selections / my goals / my personal statement *(please delete as appropriate)* to be given greater weight.

When I am dying, I would like—if my proxy and my health-care team think it is reasonable—to be cared for:

☐   at home or in a hospice

☐   ain a nursing home

☐   ain a hospital

☐   aother *(please specify)*:_____

Organ Donation

—I hereby make this anatomical gift, to take effect after my death:

I give

☐ my body

☐ any needed organs or parts

☐ the following parts _____

to

☐ the following person or institution _____

☐ the physician in attendance at my death

☐ the hospital in which I die

☐ the following physician, hospital storage bank, or other medical institution:

_____

for

☐ any purpose authorized by law

☐ therapy of another person

☐ medical education

☐ transplantation

☐ research

☐ I do not wish to make any anatomical gift from my body.

Health Care Proxy

I appoint as my proxy decision-maker(s):

_____

Name and Address

and *(optional)*

_____

Name and Address

I direct my proxy to make health-care decisions based on his/her assessment of my personal wishes. If my personal desires are unknown, my proxy is to make health-care decisions based on his/her best guess as to my wishes. My proxy shall have the authority to make all health-care decisions for me, including decisions about life-sustaining treatment, if I am unable to make them myself. My proxy's authority becomes effective if my attending physician determines in writing that I lack the capacity to make or to communicate health-care decisions. My proxy is then to have the same authority to make health-care decisions as I would if I had the capacity to make them, EXCEPT *(list the limitations, if any, you wish to place on your proxy's authority):*

I wish my written preference to be applied as exactly as possible / with flexibility according to my proxy's judgment. *(Delete as appropriate)*

Should there be any disagreement between the wishes I have indicated in this document and the decisions favored by my above-named proxy, I wish my proxy to have authority over my written statements / I wish my written statements to bind my proxy. *(Delete as appropriate)*

If I have appointed more than one proxy and there is disagreement between their wishes, _____shall have final authority.

Signed: _____   _____
          Signature   Printed Name

       _____   _____
       Address   Date

Witness: _____   _____
          Signature   Printed Name

       _____   _____
       Address   Date

Witness: _____   _____
                Signature   Printed Name

_____   _____
                Address   Date

Physician *(optional):*

I am _____'s physician. I have seen this advance care document and have had an opportunity to discuss his/her preferences regarding medical interventions at the end of life. If _____becomes incompetent, I understand that it is my duty to interpret and implement the preferences contained in this document in order to fulfill his/her wishes.

Signed: _____   _____
               Signature   Printed Name

_____   _____
                Address   Date